D0646008

Creativity
and Divine Surprise

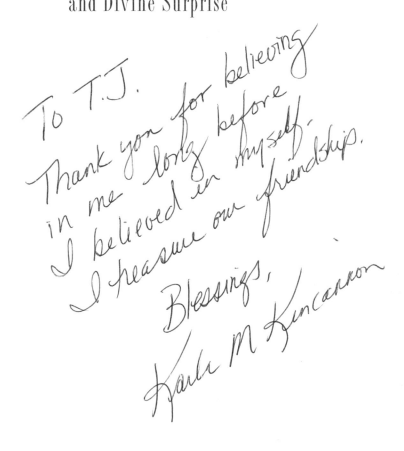

To T.J.

Thank you for believing
in me long before
I believed in myself.
I treasure our friendship.

Blessings,

Karla M Kincannon

Creativity
and Divine Surprise

Finding the Place of Your Resurrection

KARLA M. KINCANNON

Art by KARLA M. KINCANNON

UPPER
ROOM BOOKS®
NASHVILLE

CREATIVITY AND DIVINE SURPRISE
Finding the Place of Your Resurrection
Copyright © 2005 by Karla M. Kincannon
Art copyright © 2005 by Karla M. Kincannon
All rights reserved.

No part of this book may be reproduced in any manner whatsoever
without written permission of the publisher except in brief quotations embodied
in critical articles or reviews. For information, address Upper Room Books®,
1908 Grand Avenue, Nashville, Tennessee 37212.

The Upper Room® Web site: http://www.upperroom.org.

UPPER ROOM®, UPPER ROOM BOOKS® and design logos are trademarks
owned by The Upper Room®, Nashville, Tennessee. All rights reserved.

Unless otherwise noted, scripture quotations are from the New Revised Standard
Version Bible, copyright 1989 Division of Christian Education of the National
Council of the Churches of Christ in the United States of America.
Used by permission. All rights reserved.

Excerpt from "A Service of Christian Marriage I" copyright © 1979, 1980, 1985,
1989, 1992 United Methodist Publishing House. Used by permission.

Excerpt from "Somebody Loves Me Like a River," by Steve Garnaas-Holmes,
recorded by the Montana Logging & Ballet Co. on *Take the Barriers Down*, 1987.
Used by permission.

Poem "It's All about Love" copyright © 2003 by Karen Lee Turner.
Used by permission of the author.

Untitled poem by Nevin Compton Trammell © 2004.
Used by permission of the author

"Sursum Corda" excerpt, page 47, from the English translation of "Lift up your
hearts" by The English Language Liturgical Consultation.
Cover design: Charles Brock, The DesignWorks Group, Inc.
www.thedesignworksgroup.com
Cover art: istockphoto.com
Interior design: Bruce Gore / GoreStudio, Inc.
First printing: 2005

LIBRARY OF CONGRESS CATALOGING-IN-PUBLICATION DATA

Kincannon, Karla, 1953–
  Creativity and divine surprise : finding the place of your resurrection /
Karla Kincannon ; art by Karla Kincannon.
    p. cm.
  ISBN 0-8358-9812-1
  1. Creative ability—Religious aspects—Christianity. I. Title.
  BT709.5.K55 2005
  248—dc22   2005011650

Printed in the United States of America

for the One I love

Contents

CONTENTS

Acknowledgments

W riting a book, like living a life, is best done with the support of community. I am indebted to the poets, writers, artists, and theologians who are quoted in this book. Their wisdom has made my spiritual journey all the richer. A special word of thanks to Karen Lee Turner for the use of her poem "It's All about Love."

My deepest appreciation goes to Rollo May for showing me the connection between creativity and faith, to Roberta Bondi for her writings on the passions that shaped my understanding of them, to Lucia Capacchione for showing me the power of my nondominant hand, and to Thomas Keating who helped me understand my dark night.

I am especially grateful to Beth Chadsey for introducing me to art from the soul, to Rueben Job for listening and praying, and to those directees who granted me the privilege of companioning them on their spiritual journeys. Thank you for revealing God's love in the sharing of your stories.

This book would not have been written without the hospitality of the "Open Gate" and the creative synergy in those breakfasts with Carlos. You have my heartfelt thanks. The encouragement and assistance from the staff and faculty at Hiwassee College helped me more than they will ever know. I owe a big debt of gratitude to JoAnn Miller and Jeannie Crawford-Lee of Upper Room Books. Your love of this project and your thoughtful editing have delicately shaped the final work: a thousand thanks. Sarah Schaller-Linn, you have my thanks for your fine research.

Words are inadequate to express my deep gratitude to my parents for their unfailing love and support and for giving me such great brothers. Thank you to my stepchildren, their spouses, my grandchildren, nieces, and nephews for living inspiring and creative lives. To Jim Noseworthy, my husband and beloved companion on this roller-coaster ride through life, thank you for your constant love—and for waiting patiently while I found my voice.

Prologue

When we create, as when we pray, "we begin to hear the self we actually are emerging out of our shadow selves, our counterfeit selves, our pretended selves. We become aware of what is in us, the best and the worst. Our best parts, if left unlived, can be as poisonous as our worst, if left unhealed."[1] Participating in the creative act helps us to see ourselves as we are and as we might become. Like prayer, the creative act draws us into the authentic life that awaits us and into our fulfillment in God. Creativity, an essential tool for shaping the soul, provides a pathway to the fierce truth of our life. Those traveling the spiritual road who yearn for the healing of life's deepest hurts, the fulfillment of immeasurable longings, or the profound peace found only in life with God need all their creativity to complete the journey.

Though typically associated only with artists and children, creativity partially reflects the image of God within each of us. It is one strand of our divine DNA. The other strand is love, which is enormously creative. Woven together in a double helix, creativity and love compose the soul's purpose in life while providing the tools to mirror our Creator. They are the means as well as the end of the journey, the path as well as the purpose. We need both on the spiritual path: it takes creativity and love to heal the worst parts of ourselves and to live fully into the best parts. These tools of transformation carry us to union with the divine Creator, the goal of the spiritual life.

Whenever we embrace creativity and love, we come closer to embodying the person God intends us to be. Though most of us acknowledge some ability to love, many think we possess no capacity for creativity. In my ministry, I meet individuals who think they lack creativity because they cannot make art; but they can create a satisfying meal from a nearly empty pantry or conduct a business meeting in which opposing constituents work out a compromise. Creativity is so much more than art making. It is a tool for navigating through everyday experiences to find the sacred in each God-given moment. Those who believe they lack creativity have relegated it to remote regions of their life, burying it under the need for security, approval, and control. However, like love, which is stronger than death, creativity does not die; it simply waits to be unearthed and set free.

The need to rediscover our creativity is more urgent than we might think. When we exile creativity to distant corners of our existence, our ability to perceive the things of God in our life and in the life of the world radically diminishes. Without creativity we are deaf to God's call; what we are to be and do remains a conundrum. The truth of our existence lies in the heart of God, and if we cannot perceive the Divine Presence, we cannot make meaning of our days. Like the pearl of great price in Matthew's Gospel, our creativity is priceless and beyond measure.

Creativity fine-tunes our listening. By focusing our full love and attention on the creativity buried within, we train our awareness to see the Spirit's subtle stirrings over the waters of that which wants to be created in us. As we engage our creativity in the service of our spirituality, we discern the frequency of our soul's yearnings and the deeper currents of life. We hear the cries of our neighbor and know the meaning under the silence. Knitting together the known and unknown, the seen and unseen, our creativity helps us make something whole and beautiful out of the pieces of our existence. It reveals to us the truth of our soul in the place of our own resurrection.

Slipping
ever
deeper
into
the forest
each step
growing
dimmer
not knowing
how
way
opens
to
way

she
caught
her breath
felt
the breeze
heard
the trees

whisper

it's
all
about
Love

—KAREN LEE TURNER

Invitation

R.S.V.P.

*Now the LORD said to Abram, "Go from your country
and your kindred and your father's house to the land
that I will show you."*

—GENESIS 12:1

"What if the ache in your heart and all of your longings are really a longing for God?" she asked me. In the ensuing silence, that settled upon us like heavy dew on dry grass, I could hear a door opening. It was the door to my soul, and I was about to embark on a journey that would take me inward to the place of my resurrection. Through one solitary question my spiritual director gave me the key that would free me from years of stagnation in unfulfilled longing, and neither of us knew it.

If you have ever experienced an undefined longing, a pointed desire, or even a yearning to be whole, this book is an invitation to begin your search for what ultimately satisfies. For centuries people of faith have responded to an ache in the heart as a sacred longing for personal experiences of the holy. This longing has initiated thousands of pilgrimages for the purpose of connecting with mystery, finding answers to life's deepest questions, and encountering the deeply real. All pilgrimages have an inner component, and many are undertaken without physically leaving one's dwelling place. It is the inward journey that takes us to our most sacred place, the place we are closest to God and most uniquely and authentically ourselves. Here we find the fulfillment of all our longings.

19

Seeking the Place of Your Resurrection

In the early Christian era, many Celtic Christians embarked on a kind of pilgrimage called a *peregrinatio*. Unlike the pilgrimages to the Holy Land undertaken by Christians in the Middle Ages, a *peregrinatio* proposes no specific relic to see, shrine to visit, or icon to venerate. Nothing allows the pilgrim to return home with a sense of "I've been there and done that." Instead, a *peregrinatio* is a wandering into the unknown, inaugurated by the pilgrim's inner conviction of fate and fortune. Essentially a *peregrinatio* represents travel for the sake of Love, initiated and sustained by the love of God. It calls the traveler to leave all that is familiar, to let go of security and any goals or desires for life except one: to find the place of one's own resurrection.[1]

Embarking on a *peregrinatio* today may not take us to distant lands, but it will take us on a pilgrimage to discover who we are and for what purpose God created us. This transformative journey leads us to our true home in God where we give birth to our authentic self. Like our Celtic Christian ancestors, we are called to journey for the sake of Love, which requires making sacrifices, letting go of what we have worked hard to acquire. On this pilgrimage, we sacrifice such needs as those for security, control, and approval, replacing them with our love for God. As we journey toward freedom and fulfillment, only the love of God can help us reach our destination.

Beginning the Journey

Abandoning ourselves to God's mercy comprises the beginning, middle, and end of a *peregrinatio*. It does not matter that we do this perfectly; what matters is that we try. God will meet us where we are and carry us a little farther. On the inner journey we learn to trust that God wants the best for us and will, indeed, show us the way to our place of resurrection, the place where we are reborn into our true self. Beginning the inward spiritual journey initiates the pilgrimage of a lifetime. If you have a longing in your heart, you already have begun.

I would not want to commence on this inner pilgrim's journey without the benefit of insights learned from artists and from my own artistic calling. Artists point the way toward transformation on the pilgrim's path. They have made it into adulthood with their creativity intact, giving them special tools for the inner pilgrimage. Creativity shapes artists into people who perceive the unseen reality of the Divine woven into the fabric of life. With an ability to hear and see the things of God, they perceive the pulse of life underneath the surface of all activity, a pulse that most of us are prone to miss even though we search for it. These creative individuals dream dreams, see visions, and listen intently to all the layers of creation. These meaning makers assist us in making sense of the good and terrible things that happen in life. Living and breathing their creativity, artists have much to teach the pilgrim within each of us.

MILE MARKERS, SIGNPOSTS, AND TRAIL GUIDES

The following six sections in *Creativity and Divine Surprise* discuss movements in the creative process and corresponding experiences on the pilgrim's path. Most studies on the creative process include five stages of creativity: preparation, frustration, incubation, illumination, and elaboration. I have added a sixth stage—and a sixth section: encounter. Without this mysterious and mystical element, the creative process is less than it can be and less than it is intended to be.

All stages of the creative process share equal importance. We find some less intense and others more fun, but we need each one to complete the creative cycle. Once we are familiar with the stages of the creative process, they can act as sign-posts or mile markers on the spiritual journey, letting us know we have not lost our way even when we cannot see the path in front of us. Consider these stages of the creative process only as a guide not a rigid formula for traversing the inner journey. One thing is certain: if we think we know what God is going to do in our life, the Divine probably will do something different.

Though I describe how artists use their creativity, the discussion of the creative process in the following pages introduces what all individuals experience whenever they use their creativity. I hope the description of the artist's use of creativity can be a guide for you. May the artist in these pages help you understand and experience your own creative spirit so that it can serve as a tool for you on the pilgrim's journey.

When you understand your creativity, taking the time to develop it like a spiritual discipline, you forge a pathway to the Divine. Like any other spiritual discipline, creativity is only a gateway on the path where the One Who Loves Us does the guiding, the healing, and the transforming. I pray that learning to use your creativity will facilitate your inner pilgrim's journey toward wholeness and union with God. May you hear in these pages and between the words, whispers of the Creator God calling you to journey into heart and soul to the place that contains the deepest desire for who you are to be in this life. As you seek, you will find; and what you will find is the place of your own resurrection.

Unhurried Time: A Note on the Exercises

*For everything there is a season, and a time
for every matter under heaven.*

—Ecclesiastes 3:1

To encourage experience of your creativity, I invite you to engage in a creative exercise or opportunity for reflection at the end of each meditation. These exercises allow you to explore the connection between your creativity and spirituality. They are intended for ordinary people. You do not have to be a trained artist or spiritual giant to use them. If you yearn for God and desire greater awareness of God's presence in life through your creativity, you are ready. (If you are an accomplished artist, try using your nondominant hand to execute the exercises that require drawing or painting in order to receive the most from them.)

I hope the exercises will be a means of receiving God's grace as well as a source of enjoyment. These opportunities for reflection and reclaiming your creativity are intended to encourage and guide as you listen to the still small voice within. This voice connects you to the Divine Creator who calls you toward your most authentic self. Though the exercises invite travel inward, they are not intended to be therapy. Journeying on the inner path may lead to areas that need healing. If these exercises uncover such places, consider seeking out a trained therapist or spiritual director for help.

Those of you who have walked the pilgrim's path of faith for several years and are accustomed to experiencing God's presence may find the exercises beckon you into new ways of knowing God. Because most of us typically communicate with God through words, some exercises focus on images rather than words. At first you may feel awkward and clumsy attempting them. Many people feel this way initially when exploring their creativity. Usually the feeling goes away as familiarity with various artistic mediums grows. Be assured: there is no wrong way to do these exercises. Feel free to play with them or ignore them, to edit them or to repeat them, as you wish.

What to Do When Trying Something New

When experiencing something new, many of us hear an internal critical voice getting louder as we feel more vulnerable and unsure of ourselves. That critical voice often derives from an old childhood message telling us we didn't measure up or were somehow inadequate. Being chosen last for the ball team, being asked what our drawing was when it was perfectly clear to us, or competing with a sibling more adept at getting attention may have given birth to our inner critical voice. This voice frequently gets in the way of intimacy with the Divine Creator, keeping us from fully knowing the love of God.

If you find your critical voice raising its volume during one of the exercises, speak to it: tell it to go away until you are done. Also ask Christ to intercede and stand between you and the source of the critical remarks, protecting you from their barbs. If you need to address this persistent voice more directly, skip ahead to "Do Not Fear" in the section called "Encounter." It deals specifically with this aspect of being human on the spiritual path and creative journey.

Creativity as Prayer

These exercises are meant to be prayerful. As you begin each one, ask the Creating God to guide you, revealing what you need to know and do. The process is more important than the product, so pay attention to what happens within you. This is soul work.

Try to express feelings, sensations, and thoughts honestly, without censoring or criticizing them. Do not strive to produce artistic masterpieces; you will miss the heart of the experience. If instructed to draw, don't worry about being representational or making it "look good." If directed to write, don't worry about finding the perfect words. The process of expressing the deep stirrings of your soul holds more value than the finished work. You can also approach these exercises by picturing yourself getting out of the way to let God speak through you. Let the Creator work in you through your creativity, so that you become God's masterpiece.

Art from the Soul

A colleague and friend of mine the Reverend Beth Chadsey coined the phrase "art from the soul" to describe the kind of work done in these exercises. As you focus on art from the soul, you may notice your inner life—the soul—speaks in symbols. The soul is not literal-minded; therefore, it is not wise to interpret symbols in the end product literally. Noticing symbolism becomes especially significant when drawing or painting. You may need to reflect on the symbols uncovered in each exercise to discern the meaning behind them. This consideration requires the use of your imagination and a little time. The meaning may not always be self-evident. However, once you engage your imagination, the sacred becomes very clear.

Before You Begin

Here are a few suggestions for doing the exercises:

1. You will need unhurried and uninterrupted time. Most of the exercises can be done in forty-five minutes or less. A few will take longer. I like to set a timer, let the answering machine pick up the calls, and tell my family I am unavailable for anything other than an emergency. Sometimes this works; other times it does not. We all do the best we can with the circumstances life dictates.

2. Do not force yourself to do the exercises. Trust the Holy Spirit to guide you into those which will be helpful for you.

3. These exercises are immensely personal. Show them only to those who understand the inner life and have a compassionate heart. If you are working through this book with a group, sharing the finished exercises in an open and safe environment can continue the process of spiritual growth. Confidentiality is an important part of any group process. Make sure participants agree to keep to themselves all conversations shared. Remember: the soul only speaks when it feels safe.

4. You will need a few art supplies for the exercises. Each exercise lists the needed supplies. Many of the supplies work for more than one exercise. I have tried to keep the number of supplies to a minimum.

Let's get started.

May the stars light your way
and may you find the interior road.
Forward! (traditional Irish saying) [2]

Exercise

Seeing the Things of God

*Many artists have spoken of seeing things differently
while drawing and have often mentioned that
drawing puts them into a somewhat altered state
of awareness.*

—BETTY EDWARDS[3]

MATERIALS NEEDED
  journal and pen
  notepad and pencil
  one-time-use camera

A friend of mine says Christianity can be summed up in one word: *awareness*. On the spiritual path, mystics are those who are aware; their eyes have been opened to the things of God and they have "seen." They know themselves to be deeply loved by God, experiencing the Divine as the bedrock of all existence. To be truly aware of the presence of the Holy One is to be in an altered state of awareness. As pilgrims we strive for such an awareness; we yearn for it. We want to see God in the world and in our lives.

This exercise will cultivate seeing with the artist's eyes in the hope of becoming more aware. Before setting out upon a prayerful walk, take a moment to center yourself in the love of God. You may use any method that works for you, or you might try simply paying attention to your breath. As you inhale, breathe in God's love. As you exhale, let go of anything blocking that love. Simply setting the intention of being in God's love or letting go of that which blocks love can help move you into the presence of the Holy One. After a few moments of centering, ask the Spirit to guide your walking and your "seeing" in this exercise.

Take a prayerful walk and photograph evidence of God's presence at work in the world with a one-time-use camera. Where do you see God's creativity at play? Make a written record of what you photograph. Have the film processed.

When you look at the developed pictures, notice any elements that you didn't intend to be there. Notice what is missing. Don't criticize your work; simply notice. What surprises you? Often the Holy One's message comes through to us most clearly in the surprises. In your journal write about the experience of looking for God's creativity at play in the world.

Encounter

Being Met by God

He saw the Spirit of God descending like a dove.

—MATTHEW 3:16

I had just finished walking the dog in the park when I turned to look back over the open field through which we had come. In the darkening twilight at the end of an early fall day, I noticed two families with young children silhouetted against the sky. They lingered over their good-byes as if lengthening them would somehow extend the hours of daylight. I paused for a moment and watched their forms. Soaking in the beauty of the descending evening, I felt a quiet joy.

It was a holy moment, an encounter with the Divine Presence that pulsates within the circadian rhythms found in all creation. I felt one with the earth, one with those two families, with myself, and with God. For a brief moment I dwelt completely in present time, not worried about the future or stewing over the past. In the fullness of time, my awareness of God's goodness undergirding all life made everything about that moment feel whole.

Had I been in a hurry, sensing the pressure of appointments to be kept, I might have missed the encounter with joy; but I did not. I absorbed it the way a dry sponge takes in water. As I stood at the edge of the park, something about that moment seemed familiar, like renewing an acquaintance with an old friend whom you haven't seen in years. An unlocked memory floated through my mind of times as a child when the day had been so delicious I did not want it to end. I remembered the games of hide-and-seek, the sweet smell of cool earth under my sweaty body as I hid in the descending darkness. I recalled the breathless exhilaration of waiting to be found and hoping I would not be. In that moment at the edge of the park, I felt like I did as a child when my parents granted me an additional twenty minutes past bedtime to play outside: full of joy and gratitude.

A Tap on the Shoulder

In those few minutes I had an encounter with the God who loves me—who loves all of us—beyond measure. It was an act of grace, nothing I could have achieved by my own effort or willpower. I did not plan it or anticipate it. On the pilgrim's path, encounters with the holy are like that: unexpected and most often very subtle. They resemble a tap on our shoulder, a whisper in our ear, an inner voice that says, "Listen. Pay attention. There is something sacred in this moment, and it is calling your name."

Above all else, encounters are relational. When the Holy One reaches out to us as pilgrim travelers and bids us to join the dance, it is an invitation to live with the knowledge we are never alone. The One Who Loves Us accompanies us through life, wanting nothing more than for us to be whole. This Lover waits patiently for us to release our preoccupations with the things that dim our awareness of an ever-present love. Letting go of those things that cloud our vision, we experience an encounter with Sacred Love. These encounters ignite our passion for life, kindle the flame of creativity within, and invite us into a loving relationship with the Divine Creator. Every day we are encountered by the Holy One in a multitude of ways.

God continuously tries to awaken us to the Divine Presence in the world, if only we would see.

THE COMING OF DIVINE LOVE

On the first anniversary of the tragedy of September 11, 2001, people gathered to memorialize those who lost their lives in the collapse of the Twin Towers. Just as the names were read aloud at ground zero, a brisk wind began to swirl the dust at the site. I thought of the wind at Pentecost, the wind of the Holy Spirit. Persons present that day sensed the wind was imbued with spiritual significance. For those with eyes to see, the moment was transparent, a visible encounter with the presence of God called Love.

Rarely does God show up in a burning bush or strike persons blind to get their attention, although it has been known to happen. More often, an encounter with God will occur in an ordinary way, but the moment will feel exceptionally real. The Divine Lover comes to us as God came to Jesus at his baptism—gently, like a dove; and in God's coming we encounter the real and everlasting.

Most of these encounters endow us with an opportunity to enjoy the gift of the moment. For some the encounter might be in the beauty of naked trees against a winter sunset, in sunlight shining through a glass bottle of cobalt blue, or in conversations with trusted friends. For others the encounter may come through the embrace of a loved one, the smell of freshly cut roses, or a felt knowledge that God loves us. Our life is a gift. With each breath we breathe we are encountered by Love.

THE CREATIVE ENCOUNTER

Artists experience a kind of encounter in the creative act.[1] They encounter the subject of their creative expression. Light refracted through a cathedral window into a rainbow of colors moves the painter to the canvas. A song in the heart drives the musician to give it voice. A national event inspires the sculptor to mold metal into a statue, giving form to emotions felt by an entire country. Just as the pilgrim-seeker opens to a larger reality in a spiritual encounter, so too the artist opens to something beyond herself or himself in a creative encounter. That something is the very creative energy of God.

Without this encounter, a truly creative painting, sculpture, or song does not emerge. An attractive work may emerge. It may even generate income for the artist; but if not born out of God's essence—creative energy at work in the world—it is not *creative*. Without this encounter, the work of art remains less than it could have been. The encounter takes the artist— as it does the spiritual pilgrim—where she or he cannot go independently.

When I experience such an encounter as an artist, I do not so much decide to create a work of art through rational decision making as I am chosen by the piece that wants to be created. I perceive myself simply as the vehicle for expression, a servant of the work, merely cooperating with the creativity that flows through me. The produced piece of art is mine yet not mine, much the way our children are ours yet not ours. On one level they belong to us, but in the larger sense, our children belong to God, and we are simply their guardians. When I am chosen to be a guardian of a work that yearns to be created, the finished piece always seems much larger than what I intended—not larger in size but in beauty and significance.

I know my hands created it, yet I stand in humility and awe that it chose to be birthed into the world through me. I find myself asking, *Who did that?* even though I know I did. Many artists have this sense when they step back to look at their completed work. The painting is greater than the sum of its parts, and the song more magnificent than the composer had hoped.

Servants of God, Vessels of Creativity

In a similar way, the pilgrim serves as a vehicle for the expression of God in the world, a temple in which the Divine dwells on earth. The One Who Loves Us invites the pilgrim to cooperate with the work of love by allowing his or her light to shine instead of hiding it under a bushel. When we cooperate with the God who encounters us on the pilgrim's journey, we become servants of the Divine, doing the work of Love even as we allow it to be done in us. The end result always embodies greater significance than we could have accomplished on our own.

An encounter sometimes initiates creativity for the fortunate artist. Another word for this encounter is *inspiration*, something all artists seek. The word *inspiration* literally means "to breathe into," indicating inspirations come from a source beyond ourselves. The ancient Greeks thought inspiration came from the Muses, the daughters of the god Zeus, and that mortals served as receptacles for the creativity of the gods. As the Renaissance drew to a close, the belief that creativity was inherited received wide acclaim. By the end of the nineteenth century, there had been a gradual shift from the belief that all creativity came from God to a conviction that creativity was solely genetic, an inherited trait. I think the Greeks were a little closer to the truth. We are vessels for God's creativity. As we use our creativity, we conform to the Holy One's yearning for our life. When we stifle our creativity, we shut the door to God's transforming activity within us and within the world. We close the door to the fullness of love.

A SIGN OF GOD'S PRESENCE

In *The Courage to Create*, Rollo May identifies joy as the emotion that accompanies the artistic encounter.[2] Joy, the emotion I felt on that early autumn evening as I paused at the end of the park, is also what I felt as a child whose curfew had been extended to allow more time to play. Joy, sometimes born out of suffering when the One Who Loves Us has been present to the sufferer, "is the infallible sign of God's presence."[3] God is surely present in the creative encounter, because what I feel when I lose myself in writing these words or in painting a landscape is joy!

Exercise

Waking Up

> *To see a World in a grain of sand*
> *And a Heaven in a wild flower,*
> *Hold Infinity in the palm of your hand*
> *And Eternity in an hour.*

—WILLIAM BLAKE[4]

MATERIALS NEEDED
journal and pen

We are most open to the creative energies early in the morning before we get distracted by our thoughts and the pressures of the day. Once we become preoccupied with the day's duties, the creative channels close up unless we intentionally reopen them. In my experience, when I awaken without an alarm, I am an open vessel for God's creativity to flow through me. Many of my best insights come first thing in the morning even before I open my eyes. I have the habit of keeping a notepad by my bed in order to record the precious gem of a thought that soon evaporates when my feet touch the floor.

In order to access the Creator's creativity within you, try this experiment. On a day when you do not need to set the alarm, before you move, stretch, think, or get out of bed, simply notice. Notice your first image, thought, or feeling. This very passive exercise trains you to receive a divine encounter. It teaches waiting with an open mind and a receptive heart. Most of us are better at doing and giving, but we need the tools of waiting and receiving in order to encounter the presence of God and the gift of creative inspiration.

Once you have practiced awakening this way on your days off, record in your journal your first creative thoughts or images.

Do Not Fear

*You are the light of the world. A city built on a hill
cannot be hid. No one after lighting a lamp puts it
under the bushel basket, but on the lampstand, and it
gives light to all in the house. In the same way, let
your light shine before others.*

—Matthew 5:14-16

Each summer of my teen years my father planted a vegetable
garden large enough to feed the entire neighborhood. At least
it seemed that way to me, especially regarding the zucchini.
Before the new seeds and seedlings found their way into the
fertile earth, Dad assiduously prepared the ground. Readying
the soil for a new spring planting began in the fall when he
cleared the brown vegetation remaining from the summer's
harvest, allowing the land to remain fallow over the winter
months. After the last possible date for a late spring frost, Dad
opened up the dank earth with a tiller or spade, turning over
big clumps of musty dirt. Letting the freshly plowed earth sit
for a few days, he then painstakingly laid down newspaper
and mulch to minimize weeds and conserve water. With that
completed, the seeds tenderly poked into the earth were cov-
ered with nutrient-rich dirt and more mulch.

In expectation of a mouth-watering harvest, Dad nestled
the little tomato seedlings into their new beds. Tending the
garden faithfully, my father waited with hope and anticipation
for a new crop of summer vegetables. I am amazed at how

much work went into this summer garden even before the first seed was planted.

When I think of how God works in the life of the pilgrim, I remember the tireless work my dad put into preparing the soil for his garden. Just as he patiently readied the earth, so too God prepares the pilgrim's heart to receive an encounter with Divine Love. Seasons before we become aware of the movement of God's love in our life, and long before we see any evidence of the fruit of that love, seeds of faith, hope, and love already are growing in our pilgrim heart.

THE GRACE THAT GOES BEFORE

John Wesley, the founder of Methodism, called God's loving groundwork *prevenient grace*. It is the love that goes before us from the moment of our conception, preparing us to receive a fuller portion of God's transforming presence. It works in our life long before we decide to become spiritual pilgrims and makes us ready to welcome an encounter with the Divine Lover. This Divine Lover yearns to guide us into wholeness and joy. Prevenient grace searches us out and cultivates awareness of its presence within. We do not seek it, yet it finds us.

As we become aware of the love that seeks and finds, sometimes, rather than feeling comforted by its presence, we find it annoying or frightening. If we have set our own agenda but God has something else in mind, we feel cornered. When part of us, for whatever reason, chooses not to be healed, we feel hounded to death by the love that wants our wholeness. Pilgrims who fear making sacrifices on this journey may find the Holy Spirit's hot breath on the back of the neck anything but comforting. A truth not often articulated in religious circles is that we all have to let go of things to make room for God. As seed-planting time draws closer, fearful pilgrims intent on holding on to their own agenda may be found echoing the words of the psalmist, "Where can I go from your spirit? Or where can I flee from your presence?" (Ps. 139:7). The pilgrim's journey toward union with God does not always feel good; it can be downright scary at times.

FEAR AND CONTROL ON THE INNER JOURNEY

I heard a physician explain that fear diminishes communication among the cells in our body. Fear also inhibits communication in other areas of our life. It can keep us from welcoming the stranger and from being in communion with God. Fear can potentially block divine love. The Holy One is not deaf to our cries when we are afraid; rather, we do not always hear God. In the presence of fear, we can close down, unable to receive the Divine's abundant love. Of course, not all fear is bad. The body's fight-or-flight response to fear works to keep us safe; however, fear becomes unhealthy when we feel afraid for no apparent reason.

On the spiritual journey, fear wears many disguises. Often it resembles control. As pilgrims, we may be afraid to let go and let God take charge. We think we know what is best for us, and if we could convince the Almighty of that fact, our life would run smoothly. According to Parker Palmer, this attitude characterizes the functional atheist, a person who trusts in human abilities above God's grace. We all have at least one corner of life where we would rather our ego be in charge than let the Creator meddle in our affairs. Our hard-won independence, a necessary step toward becoming a healthy adult, is very difficult to surrender. However, on the spiritual journey, the pilgrim must surrender the ego because the ego cannot make the journey inward to our deepest, truest self.

Relinquishing our ego can frighten us because at some level we feel like the sky may fall. We worry that God's plans conflict with our deepest desires. What will become of our dreams and goals if we surrender to God's yearning for our life? Though this fear might remain unexamined, buried under the surface of our life, it shapes the way we live. We may even fear we will cease to exist if transformed by God's desires. Our ego does not always go gently into that dark night.

Those of us who possess intimate knowledge of this fear do not trust God and cannot believe the Holy One wants the best for us. Ironically, only through letting go of the ego do we really live. As we are transformed into the person God intends us to be, we find the place of our resurrection. Our light shines brilliantly even as our heart's deepest yearning is fulfilled.

Fear can block our growth on the pilgrim's path, keeping us from becoming transformed vessels of God's light and love. Marianne Williamson suggests we may feel trepidation on the pilgrim's journey because we are afraid to let our light shine. She writes, "Our deepest fear is not that we are inadequate. Our deepest fear is that we are powerful beyond measure. It is our light, not our darkness, that frightens us. . . . And as we let our own light shine, we unconsciously give other people permission to do the same. As we're liberated from our own fear, our presence automatically liberates others."[5] Part of a pilgrim's work on the journey is to overcome our fear in order to serve as a beacon of liberation for others imprisoned in the darkness of despair, injustice, alienation, and fear.

FINDING ONE VOICE, LOSING ANOTHER

As an artist, I know about the fear of letting my light shine. It is called the fear of finding my voice. When I'm inspired by a subject, a craving to create gushes up within me like an artesian well. I search for a way to recreate the encounter in a style authentically and uniquely mine. The more deeply felt the experience, the greater the likelihood of breaking into a cold sweat because it feels as if I am putting my private life on display. This fear potentially silences my voice and sends me scrambling for a bushel basket under which to hide.

When it comes to artistic expression, the trepidation around letting my light shine manifests from a critical voice within. I call this critical voice my gremlin, and it can make me believe I have nothing of value to offer the world. My gremlin has told me not to take risks because I won't be good enough. At the sound of its voice my creative juices freeze.

Most artists hear these inner critical voices. The voices tell lies, using all necessary means to keep us afraid of finding our own voice. They tell us we have no talent. They intimate something bad will happen if we express our creativity. Our gremlins play on our unexamined fears, fostering self-doubt. They hiss from the bleacher seats in our mind, "Creativity is dangerous. You must be crazy to try that! You'll be rejected if you try something innovative." Born of past wounds, our fearful inner gremlin tries to protect us from hurt by silencing our creative voice.

When my nephew was three years old, he spent one entire morning making hand puppets. I watched as he lost himself in sheer delight. Adorning paper bags with stickers and glitter and embellishing them with scribbles from colorful markers, he couldn't produce the puppets fast enough. Breathless with enthusiasm, he sighed, "Oh, Aunt Karla, thank you for bringing this." When his seven-year-old sister came home that afternoon suffering from an upsetting episode at school, he rushed to show her his beautiful creations. Passing along her bad mood, she said to him, "They aren't very good." From that moment on, the puppets he had so enjoyed were cast aside. He wanted nothing further to do with them. Valuing his sister's approval more than his own creativity, he let go of that which he had loved passionately only moments before.

Most of us had similar experiences as children. We may have shown one of our beautiful creations to someone who did not cherish it the way we did. Perhaps it was rejected or ignored, left in a pile of clutter to gather dust. We may have been told "people aren't blue" by someone trying to be helpful. This kind of criticism, even though unintentional, can kill a child's creative spirit even as it radically diminishes our creativity as adults. Instead of experiencing our creativity as "very good," the way the Creator God perceives creativity, we learn to devalue it. We believe it to be suspect, unworthy of our love and attention. At a very young age we lose our creative voice and find our critical voice.

THE FALSE SELF

Most everyone, including the spiritual pilgrim, has an inner critical voice. Hurtful incidents are not confined to childhood drawings; they occur around many kinds of self-expression from our earliest years. Forgetting words to a song in a school play and the subsequent teasing by our classmates can have the same effect. A dismissed hug or harshly criticized behavior can dwarf our development. As children we cannot differentiate between what we do and who we are. When our acts are not received well or not received at all, we think something is wrong with us. Because our survival depends on the love of others, we adapt. We bury the part of ourselves that does not meet the approval of others along with the joy of creating. The pride of accomplishment and the desire to share ourselves with others also get buried because we lack wisdom to discern between our behavior and the essence of our spirit. These experiences make us fearful of expressing our uniqueness and send us scurrying to protect ourselves from hurt or embarrassment in the future.

We may not even remember our past hurts, but our bodies and our emotions remember. Although wounds we experienced as children may not have been inflicted intentionally, they still left their mark. When current circumstances remind us of events we once experienced as dangerous or hurtful, the same feelings emerge with impact. Our critical voice, seeing an opening, steps up to bat: "Play it safe. Don't risk it," it says. This voice perpetuates fear and keeps us paralyzed without our knowing why. On the pilgrim's path this is the voice of the false self.

The false self wants to do things its way, separate from God's desires for us, because it lives in fear. It is the functional atheist in each of us. Claiming authenticity, this small, superficial self masquerades as our true self. It casts a shadow on our authentic self, dimming our brilliance. The false self has tragically forgotten we are made in the Creator's image. Suffering from dementia of the soul, it no longer remembers that our creativity connects us to God. Our false self, lost in self-sufficiency, believes it does not need God's creative love. In truth, our false self needs a whole lot of love.

The Voice of Love

Whether we are encountering God on the pilgrim's path or finding our voice in the creative process, fear sometimes overtakes us. The only remedy I know for our fears is love: perfect love casts out all fear. Love opens the channels for healthy communication among the cells of our bodies. It builds bridges between individuals and nations. Love is the bond between the Creator and all of creation; it holds us together. Whether we are afraid to surrender our ego or afraid to use our creative voice, love is the only cure.

Listening for the voice of God who is Love helps us defeat our fears. The Divine's voice differs from the voice of our inner gremlin. We recognize God's voice because it tells us we are loved and accepted as we are: trembling, anxious, and fearful creatures. God speaks as our Beloved, embracing us in a way that transforms us into new beings who are whole, beautiful, and loving. The Holy One's voice passionately urges us to love ourselves as God loves us—deeply, endlessly, with the yearning of one lover for another. If we listen to this voice with the ears of the heart, little by little we will have learned to love the frightened part of ourselves. Like a sculptor, we will have chipped away at the frozen fear to reveal the beautiful creation inside.

Thank God for perfect love that casts out all fear.

Exercise

Fear Is a Four-Letter Word

> *You formed us in your image*
> *and breathed into us the breath of life.*
> *When we turned away, and our love failed,*
> *your love remained steadfast.*

— THE UNITED METHODIST BOOK OF WORSHIP[6]

MATERIALS NEEDED
journal and pen
18" x 24" drawing paper
colored markers or crayons

I am my own worst enemy; my interior critical voice shows no mercy. For twenty-five years I have worked to replace interior criticisms with positive affirmations. To change a critical message, first we must notice it.

This exercise will help you begin to identify your negative inner chatter. Before you start, prayerfully ask the Spirit of God to be present, guiding you through this exercise. Take your time and be loving toward yourself.

Think of the times when the critical voice within you spoke loudly, casting a shadow of self-doubt across a deep desire. What message did you hear in your head? How did the inner criticism misrepresent a truth about you? What words did the critical voice use to keep you stuck and unhappy? (If you have difficulty identifying your inner critical gremlin, spend a day or two listening to your own inner self-talk.)

If you could personify this critical voice, what would it look like? Using crayons or colored markers, make a picture of him or her. You can make it funny, scary, childlike, or ugly. It is up to you. There is no wrong way to portray this creature.

Once you have drawn this critical voice, have a conversation with it on paper. You may want to ask its name. If it does not reveal one, give it a name. In ancient days, naming the demon gave the person power over it. The same holds true today.

Writing in your journal, use your dominant hand and ask the voice questions: Who are you? Where did you come from? What do you want from me? These are good for starters. Using your nondominant hand to write its answers, allow the critical voice to respond to your questions. Don't worry if the process is slow or the writing sloppy. In this exercise, the non-dominant hand can open the doors to deep wisdom. (Lucia Capacchione, in *The Power of Your Other Hand*, explores in depth the process of using our nondominant hand to access deep inner wisdom.[7])

Many of us hear more than one critical message from our inner gremlin. You may want to repeat this exercise for each negative message, bringing to the light of day the criticisms that keep you from your authentic self and your creative voice.

A word of advice: You may not want to give creative form to all the critical messages in one sitting. You can repeat this exercise over days, weeks, or even months.

Glimpses of the True Self

You will know the truth, and the truth will make you free.

—JOHN 8:32

Listening to my body has taught me much about myself. Early in my career, I noticed whenever I approached a certain solitary task, my neck began to throb with pain. After experiencing the pain for what felt like the one hundredth time, I said aloud in exasperation, "What is this pain in my neck?!" Hearing my own words illuminated the truth for me. My body was trying to get my attention to reveal my true feelings about the task in front of me: it was a royal pain in the neck! What my mind and emotions hesitated to admit, my body broadcast loudly. Like a child who sees the truth and announces it no matter how ill-timed her remark might be for the social comfort of those within earshot, the body speaks the truth. It does not lie; neither does the creative process.

Creativity is honest. It comes from a place deep within that does not know how to be deceptive. By participating in the creative process, a pathway forms to inner wisdom, leading to insights about the nature of our true self. One layer at a time, the creative process gently peels back the camouflage that has accumulated over years of living. This camouflage, configured out of past hurts and failures, hides the beauty of our true identity. When artists experience an encounter in the creative process, a glimpse of the true self accompanies it.

During a workshop I led on the creative process and the spiritual journey, one individual received such an encounter. Deeply affected by a terrorist bombing, she struggled to come to terms with such a senseless act of violence. Though she considered art frivolous and had not painted since grade school, she dutifully followed the instructions for "art from the soul." Using her intuition to guide the placement of paint on canvas, she dabbed color here and there without a preconceived notion of what she was creating. At the end of the exercise, she stepped back for the first time to view her painting. Unaware of creating any image at all, she gasped with surprise as she saw in her painting an abstract image of the weeping Christ standing in the midst of an explosion. Her painting helped her connect the suffering of God's people to the suffering of Christ. It proved to be a powerfully honest revelation about her compassion for the victims of the bombing.

Knowing God, Knowing Self

The self-revelations the artist receives through the creative process are akin to those the pilgrim experiences through faithful prayer. Often healing, these insights provide what we need for our continued growth. Whether through creativity or prayer, probing the deep mysteries of our being brings us face-to-face with the Divine who creates and sustains all life. This is the truth of Christian mysticism: knowledge of self and knowledge of God are one.

When I was fourteen, the Christian educator at my church asked members of our youth fellowship group to consider committing our lives to God. He explained we could not know everything about our Creator, but we would learn more as our faith grew. He also said maturity would help us understand more about who we are. While we would never know everything about God or ourselves, new knowledge in one area promised new knowledge in another. He invited us to enter into a dynamic relationship with our Creator by taking this first step on our spiritual journey.

The truth I heard at age fourteen echoes in the writings of the fourteenth-century Italian mystic Catherine of Siena, who explored the connection between self-knowledge and knowledge of God. Catherine describes prayer as a cell of self-knowledge, recognizing the pathway to God is also a pathway to knowing oneself. She writes, "For knowing only ourselves, or wanting to know God without knowing ourselves, would not be a knowledge grounded in truth."[8] So intimate is the relationship between knowledge of God and knowledge of self that as we grow in one area, we grow in another.

We do not undertake this journey of self-discovery alone. God invites us to the journey and accompanies us along the way, guiding every step. This pilgrimage always leads to the Truth, and the Truth sets us free. In the words of my mother, "God's love is the only truth there is." It is always and only God's love that frees us.

CREATIVITY AND PRAYER

Creativity and prayer allow us to see the truth about ourselves. Whether painting or praying, I learn about myself and areas of my life that need God's healing. Painting offers guidance and helps to heal the hurts of the past, in much the same way prayer does. Through an unending process of self-discovery, creativity and prayer move us into wholeness. They afford an encounter with self-knowledge and lead to the joyful truth of our existence.

Creativity and prayer direct us inward to the image of God within. Through these means we come to know the place inside that remains whole and holy no matter how our years of living may have twisted our life out of shape. Both processes proceed from deep honesty, similar to the honesty of childhood, before anyone injured us or told us we were unlovable, before we knew how to pretend to be someone we were not. Prayer and creativity serve to reveal how old hurts have shaped us so that God might free us from the power those former wounds may hold.

THE BEGINNINGS OF THE FALSE SELF

Even in the best of families, children's needs cannot be met all the time. When a child's need goes unmet, an emotional wound is sustained and stored in the body. This phenomenon belongs to the human condition; it happens to all of us. In order to survive the original hurt, we learn to wrap the wound with a layer of protection. Our defenses develop to buffer the pain from the primary unmet need and to shield us from future hurts. According to Thomas Keating in *Invitation to Love*, a secondary need develops over time to counter the original wound. This secondary need starts us looking for happiness in all the wrong places. Keating writes, "These emotional programs for happiness start out as needs, grow into demands, and can finally become 'shoulds.'"[9] They become our motivation for living and are the beginnings of the false self.

An original wound does not have to be the result of severe abuse or trauma. We are all vulnerable as children. Children cannot filter out strong emotions or discern appropriate responsibility for events. They experience life as if they are at the center of it because their defenses are not fully formed. For example, a child in the room with parents who argue heatedly cannot discern at whom the anger is directed. Though the parents may be oblivious to the presence of their offspring, the child takes the anger to heart, believing he or she is to blame. It never occurs to the parents that their offspring might interpret himself or herself as the target of their anger. In this situation, the child's basic needs for love and security are not met, and a wound develops.

In order to survive the pain of an unmet need, the child wraps the wound in a layer of protection called a defense. Our defenses help us survive life, but they can get in the way as we mature, preventing us from knowing the abundant life God wants to give us. The child in our example begins to equate happiness with avoiding these kinds of "dangerous," angry situations. When faced with similar situations, this child will move instinctually into a protective mode, not wanting to be hurt again. He or she may shut down emotionally in the face of confrontation or try to please others in an effort to keep them from being angry. The secondary need, to avoid the hurt of anger, becomes the child's motivation to find happiness.

What Keating calls our "emotional programs for happiness" take on power as we mature. Our secondary need becomes the unconscious driving force behind our life. Having forgotten the initial wound, now hidden in the recesses of our mind and the cells of our body, we look for love and happiness in all the wrong places. The original wound from our unmet basic needs and the resulting secondary need shape the way we see life. They can make us feel we need to control all situations or believe the world is out to get us. They can drive us to accumulate wealth in an attempt to be secure or cause us to react to most circumstances with hostility. They can shape us into people pleasers or perpetual victims in life.

Over time, these ways of trying to find happiness control us and become our false self. Like an addiction, the false self's search for love and happiness becomes more restrictive, diminishing our freedom and our joy. It takes us on wild-goose chases that promise only short-term satisfaction, not deep abiding joy. The false self is the part of us that becomes misshapen through our years of living. Desperately in need of God's love, it remains oblivious to its poverty. The false self operates out of confidence in its ability to achieve love and happiness by its own merit. The problem is that our false self cannot make the journey to our deepest center where our true self resides. Until we dismantle the false self, we will not reach the place of our own resurrection.

DISMANTLING THE FALSE SELF

Through creativity and prayer, the false self begins to unravel. This is not somber work, and we do not achieve it by our own endeavor. We give our consent and God does the work. We can cooperate with God, but on our own we cannot undo the false self. Meister Eckhart remarked, "The soul will bring forth Person if God laughs into her and she laughs back to him."[10] Dismantling the false self is not a punishment; it is a joyful and adventurous journey that leads to new life. Our Creator desires only to deepen our joy and happiness and knows we will not be satisfied until we rest in the love of the Divine.

On the pilgrim's path, the recovery of our creativity and the use of faithful prayer enable God to put the false self to rest. With the dismantling of the false self, we find freedom in the truth of our existence.

Exercise

In Search of Freedom

> *Hear my prayer:*
> *help me*
> *let go*
> *of what's*
> *not*
> *there*

—NEVIN COMPTON TRAMMELL[11]

MATERIALS NEEDED
18" x 24" drawing paper
colorful markers

Pausing to take stock of where we have been in life assists us in moving forward. Examination of past events allows us to shed unwanted emotional and spiritual baggage. When left unexamined, such baggage inhibits our moving forward in life. As we reflect on significant past events and periods of inner activity, we gain new understanding of the way the Divine Lover works in our life. Glimpses of insight reveal how God shapes us.

Before you begin, prayerfully ask your Holy Guide to be present to you through this exercise. Imagine your life as an intentional journey to discover who God has created you to be. Though you may not yet have found your place of resurrection, draw a map of your pilgrimage. To accomplish this, you may want to think of a continent or other land mass as a metaphor for your life. How much have you already explored? How much territory is yet uncharted?

Designate each significant event in your life—both the joyful and painful ones—as a landmark, town, or camp site, and name each one. For example, if your birth story is a happy one, plot a city on your map and call it "Joyful Tidings." If you have experienced a difficult time of trial, you might draw a valley named "Valley of Dry Bones." Use your creativity and imagination to draw the pilgrimage to the place of your own resurrection.

Once you've drawn the map, use a dotted line to connect the landmarks and cities in order of occurrence. Then revisit each point of interest, pausing to remember who you understood yourself to be and what image you had for God at that time in your life. You may want to devise a key to your map with this information. If so, list each town or landmark and beside it write a brief description of yourself at that age along with a description of how you understood the image of God.

When finished, give thanks to your Guiding Light for directing you on this journey toward your place of resurrection.

Preparation

Feed the Hunger

As a deer longs for flowing streams,
so my soul longs for you, O God.

—PSALM 42:1

Artists hunger for creativity the way spiritual pilgrims hunger for God. This yearning arises from the same source for both the artist and the pilgrim. It is the Divine Lover at work within the soul, drawing the pilgrim and the artist into deeper intimacy. Satisfying this longing pulls us into a journey on a road paved with discipline.

At the foundation of the creative process and the authentic spiritual life lies grace-filled discipline. Although we associate the spiritual disciplines with the journey of faith, we're often surprised to learn that creativity also requires discipline. Fiction perpetuates the stereotype of the lazy but impulsive artist. Discipline cannot be avoided in creativity or spirituality if either is to bear fruit. There are no shortcuts for the artist or the pilgrim. To reach the end, we all have to start at the beginning using the building blocks of disciplined practice. For the artist, a work of art communicated with others signifies completion of the creative process. For the pilgrim, fulfillment of the spiritual journey is union with God.

According to Graham Wallas's theory on creativity in *Understanding Creativity*, preparation is the first stage of the creative process.[1] More often than not, preparation in the form of discipline begins many creative works. Though every artist longs for an encounter to initiate creativity which makes the creative process feel effortless, this does not always occur. Sometimes the encounter takes place in one of the later stages of the creative process. Without the discipline of showing up each day at the writer's desk, the piano, or the easel, the chance of producing a creative work of art greatly diminishes. Frequently discipline becomes the very tool that opens the door to an encounter between the artist and the subject.

PATIENCE

The preparation stage of the creative process involves gathering information about the problem to be solved or the challenge presenting itself. Whether challenged to house America's homeless or paint like Picasso, the process of preparation remains the same. With an open mind and open heart, curiosity is the order of the day. The preparation stage invites us to inquire, reframe questions, and try on various perspectives without forcing a premature answer. Using the questions from Journalism 101 class—who, what, when, where, why, and how—provides a good place to begin. In the preparation stage, the artist tries to empty out preconceptions. Facing the presenting challenge with a beginner's mind, the artist remains open to all possible solutions. At this stage of the creative process, artists cease looking for the right answer and simply explore, trusting the answer will come eventually. In the words of Rainer Maria Rilke in *Letters to a Young Poet*, now is the time to "be patient toward all that is unsolved in your heart and to try to love the *questions themselves* like locked rooms and like books that are written in a very foreign tongue. . . . *Live* the questions now."[2] "Living the questions" describes the attitude needed at the beginning of each creative endeavor.

Preparation takes time. When I was a child, getting ready for vacation always took more time than I could bear. The packing seemed endless because I was excited about reaching our destination. Once on the road, travel turned into an eternity. "Are we there yet?" became the plaintive chorus from the backseat. Preparation for any creative activity takes more time than we think it will: the canvas has to be primed, the supplies purchased, the piano tuned, the dance rehearsed, and new skills learned. All these activities require patience and time if they are to be done well. Without the fruit of the Spirit called patience, the landscape never gets painted and the poem remains locked in unarticulated thoughts.

Losing patience nips creativity in the bud, preventing it from unfolding. The poet Rilke writes:

Being an artist means . . . ripening like the tree which does not force its sap and stands confident in the storms of spring without the fear that after them may come no summer. It does come. But it comes only to the patient, who are there as though eternity lay before them . . . *patience* is everything![3]

The overeager individual, tempted to skip ahead of the preparation stage, often plunges headlong into the later stages of the creative process. This actually bogs down the process, making it necessary for the artist to revisit the preparation stage before completing the work of art.

Impatience presents a stumbling block on the pilgrim's journey too. We do not become a saint or mystic overnight; the journey to our true self takes years. In the time-consuming work of each day, we are transformed by God. Like apples slowly ripening, spiritual maturity and creativity cannot be hurried or forced. "*Patience* is everything."

As an artist, I work at being patient; it is not my nature. If I can make the activity in which I am engaged fun, my patience increases. My parents acted on this reality when they presented my brothers and me with travel games to stop the whining on those long vacation trips of my childhood. As an artist and writer, when I begin to whine about the length of time needed to prepare a canvas or research an article, I allow myself to brainstorm.

AMBIGUITY AND UNCERTAINTY

Brainstorming is sheer play for many artists. It allows us to entertain potential solutions without censoring any of them. It teaches us to hold all possibilities in open consideration, to coexist with the ambiguity and paradox inherent in all creative endeavors. In today's world where change occurs rapidly and certainties move in constant flux, gaining comfort with ambiguity makes for artful living. Most of us, preferring the predictable and orderly, resist ambiguity and even shut down in the face of major uncertainty. Our world needs people who can hold divergent viewpoints without closing their hearts or minds. Such people envision possibilities for a peaceful existence of differing ideas and diverse individuals.

Most artists tolerate ambiguity to a greater degree than the general population because we deal with it regularly. The preparation stage of the creative process shows the artist how to embrace ambiguity as a challenge, to view it with excitement rather than with fear, as opportunity rather than a threat. Moving through the preparation stage, the artist learns to trust that a solution eventually will materialize. New creations come out of uncertainties. Like explorers, artists hold onto the hope and promise of potential fulfilled. Traveling to the edge of life where the known and unknown meet, we often catch a glimpse of the Great Creator at work in the possibilities of what is not yet—but soon to be.

The artist's willingness to experience the unknown in the creative process can teach the pilgrim to welcome and embrace the uncertainty inherent on the spiritual journey. As pilgrims, we may trust God's promises but remain anxious over how they manifest in our life. When God calls us to begin a pilgrimage, to leave the familiar for that which is unseen, looking to the artist can give some assistance on how to make the journey. Hope sustains the artist beckoned forward into what is yet to be. Hope holds the promise of a solution to the creative process. Hope assists survival during the darkest uncertainties. Since much of our journey as pilgrims requires placing one foot in front of the other even when we do not see the road beneath us, hope is an essential tool for the road. Developing hope takes work and preparation.

The Disciplines

Preparation for the pilgrim's journey comes through spiritual disciplines. The disciplines facilitate an attitude of hope even as they teach us how to trust God on the journey to the place of our resurrection. In particular, the inward disciplines of prayer and contemplation reveal what the artist learns from the preparation stage in the creative process. They teach us how to remain open and receptive when confronted with ambiguity and uncertainty. Keeping our hearts and minds open in the face of the unknown is the essence of hope.

Faithful prayer develops within us deeper degrees of hope and trust. When we pray, we act in the hope that the Keeper of Promises will answer our prayer. Though unsure as to the when and how our prayer will be answered, we trust an answer will come. Just as exercising muscles builds strength, praying promotes confidence in the Keeper of Promises. Prayer enables us to exhale into the arms of God, trusting the Divine Lover to hold us tenderly.

As prayer grows deeper it requires fewer words. Eventually we may move from articulated thought into mere Presence, from the prayer of petition to the prayer of contemplation. Here we rest securely in the Divine Presence. Here we learn the language of silence. As we migrate into the unfamiliar and the unknown, the silence brings us face-to-face with Mystery. Moving beyond logical knowing into a knowing based on pure faith, we are in a state of grace. Though hundreds of uncertainties in life surround us, the awareness of divine love gained through contemplation creates peace deep within our being. Contemplation enables us to face whatever is unclear with hope that a way will open and clarity will come.

Neither the pilgrim nor the artist can avoid uncertainty and ambiguity. If we hunger for creativity or hunger for God, we must learn to navigate through uncertain times. Through the patient discipline of showing up for prayer or showing up to create, the pilgrim and the artist engender the hope and trust needed to continue on their paths. Only in walking through life's ambiguities do we find that for which we search in the meeting of the known and unknown.

Exercise

Following Through

> The Disciplines are God's way of getting us into the
> ground; they put us where he can work within us and
> transform us.

—RICHARD FOSTER[4]

MATERIALS NEEDED

8 ½" x 11" or larger drawing paper
watercolors or tempera paints
container of water
paintbrush
paint rag

Delayed gratification helps us to be patient. If I am feeling impatient, I promise to reward myself with a walk in the woods, a chocolate chip cookie, or time to listen to my favorite CD. I use whatever it takes to keep me in the moment so that I can create. Most of the time, delayed gratification works well; so does prayer.

In this exercise you are going to make a visual prayer. *Mandala* is a Sanskrit word meaning "circle." Mandalas are visual prayers contained in a circle. You are going to create one. Before you start, promise yourself a small reward when you finish: listening to five minutes of your favorite music, taking a walk, or telephoning a friend.

Purchase a children's set of watercolors or tempera paints. Most watercolor sets come with a brush, but you may want to purchase an inexpensive one of your own choosing. If you like more vibrant colors, use tempera paints; watercolors tend to produce a softer appearance.

You'll need a container of water, an old rag to clean your brush, and a sheet of paper.

To begin, ask the Creator God to guide you in creating your mandala. Draw a circle with a circumference that takes in almost the entire page. Use a dinner plate or pot lid as a template if you wish. Prayerfully represent your current life circumstance and your reaction to it. How do you feel about your life? Are you happy, struggling, sad, content? How do you think God relates to your life situation? What do you want God to do in your life? Do not try to paint images unless that feels appropriate. Many mandalas consist of only color and pattern. Once again, it is important to stay present to the process.

Create as you feel led. When you finish, be sure to follow through with your reward.

Wholehearted Listening

Be still, and know that I am God!

—Psalm 46:10

Artists know much about listening. Wanting to hear an inner voice, something more than mindless chatter to guide them through the creative process, artists wait for inspiration and a solution to the creative challenge. As they wait, they listen. It has been said that artists listen for their muse to speak. Whether listening for a muse, an inspiration, an inner voice, or a creative encounter, the key to the listening is expectation. Artists expect to hear that for which they listen. Just as the pilgrim trusts the promise that seeking will lead to finding, the artist trusts that listening will lead to a creative solution.

Listening with the Senses

Both the artist and the pilgrim find listening a difficult task in our noisy culture. Only the novice listener considers it effortless. A myriad of seductive voices compete for our attention. Family, friends, and society all place expectations upon us, which—for good or ill—define who we are. The advertising industry cries out, imploring us to buy products that promise to make us smarter, sexier, wealthier, more popular and powerful. Even if we quiet these outer voices, the inner chatter of replayed conversations keeps the silence necessary for creative listening at the door of our hearts, waiting for entry.

It is easy to listen to inner babble and external voices. However, only in diving below the surface of our days do we taste the silence that renews and transforms. Only then do we experience the silence out of which God speaks a creative word.

Artists practice listening as a regular part of the creative process. Like a spiritual discipline that opens the pilgrim to God, listening opens the artist to creativity. In the preparation stage of the creative process, the artist listens for anything that has possibility, anything that might contain a seed of creative insight. Like hungry children who trust their parents to give them bread instead of stones, artists listen with faith that they will feast on the gift of creativity.

Artists listen with their intuition. They listen with their senses. The fragrance of baking bread could inspire sketches of wheat being cut and crushed into flour. The discord of noisy traffic might develop into a documentary on air pollution or a contemporary symphony. Artists listen with all their senses because creative insight might be lurking just beyond earshot or beyond one's line of sight. It could even be found in the next mouthful of warm bread.

Artists can find what they yearn for only in the present moment, and the discipline of listening teaches how to stay open to the present. Our senses help focus us in the here and now. Seeing, hearing, tasting, touching, smelling, and receiving a hunch all happen in present time—the only place we receive inspiration. Creativity only occurs in the present, not in the past or in the future. In the here and now inspiration meets the artist with the invitation to create.

God comes to the pilgrim in the present moment too. As pilgrims, we may remember God's faithful actions in the past and hope for God's saving activity in our future, but we experience God in the present. When we taste the bread of Communion, feel the life-giving waters of baptism, or listen for the Word of God in silence, we meet God in the present moment.

A Lutheran friend's goddaughter had been to the Communion rail many times in her short life. By the age of three, she had tasted the bread and smelled the wine weekly since her infant baptism. She had heard "This is the body and blood of Christ given for you" spoken over the bread and cup numerous times. One evening at home when guests were expected, the little girl watched her parents pour wine for dinner. Her curiosity drew her closer. Climbing into the dining room chair, she asked if she could smell the red liquid in the glass. Her mother consented, carefully supervising her daughter. As the young girl inhaled the fragrance, she said with awe, "Mommy, it smells like Christ!" Children recognize our senses as a gift through which we experience God in the here and now.

LISTENING WELL

Listening with our senses teaches us as pilgrims to be open to God in whom all things are possible. The more of ourselves we bring to each moment— the more senses we use—the greater the possibility of hearing what God says to us. Since every aspect of life reveals God's presence, we must learn to tune to God's frequency in the world and in our lives through the act of listening.

Most of us listen only halfheartedly. Listening with minds preoccupied, thinking about the to-do list, our thoughts focus on where we must be in the next hour. Preconceived expectations determine what we actually hear. We listen to our lover as if we already know what she or he will say. We hear political debates having previously decided how to vote on the issue. We even listen for God anticipating the words the Holy

One will speak. This is not truly listening. To listen well we must be open to all possibilities, a difficult state of awareness to achieve. It takes courage to listen well. Letting go of what we expect to hear, we run the risk of hearing nothing—or at least nothing familiar. To listen well requires emptying ourselves of preconceptions, a daunting and threatening task.

Rather than do the hard work of listening, many prefer to hear the familiar voice of the ego. It speaks in certitudes and sees life in black and white. We would rather listen to the predictable voice of our false self that sounds indisputable and all-knowing but never leads us to abundant life. Too often we choose the clamor of familiar voices over the unpredictable whisper of the Holy Spirit, whose voice sounds surprisingly new and asks only for our love.

LISTENING AS PRAYER

Listening for the voice of the Spirit, for the inner voice, involves an act of holy obedience. The word *obedient* comes from the Latin word *audire,* which means "to listen."[5] Listening well goes beyond intellectual activity. Wholehearted listening requires bringing our whole self—body, mind, heart, and spirit—into the act of listening.

The ancient Hebrews understood the heart to be the center of the entire person, the nucleus of emotion, will, and intellect. Wholehearted listening invites deep listening, not the selective listening a parent uses with a babbling three-year-old child. It requires suspension of premature judgments, allowing the pilgrim to receive new information and embrace new possibilities. Wholehearted listening teaches us to pay attention to all facets of life with the expectation that God can come to us in the most unlikely ways.

The artist listens wholeheartedly in the midst of the creative process. Though listening underlies the creative process from start to finish, it is as intrinsic to the preparation stage as prayer is to being with God. Without the ability to listen, both the preparation stage and the creative process cease to exist.

Listening lies the heart of the pilgrim's journey. If we are deaf to God, the journey to the place of our resurrection never begins. Listening defines the work of prayer; it helps transform us into the person our Creator intended us to be all along. Much like musicians educating themselves to identify notes played by specific instruments in an orchestra, when we pray we learn to hear God's note in and among all the competing sounds in the symphony of life. This kind of prayer assists in detecting God's presence in the midst of life's ordinary and extraordinary events. It cultivates within us an ear to hear the Divine in the cry of the poor, the plea of the prisoner, and the sigh of the stranger. We discover—both in the beauty and in the pain—our Creator's creativity at work.

The practice of distinguishing God's voice exposes our inner chatter for what it really is: our fearful, false self that hesitates to trust the promises of the Divine Lover. Listening prayer and the preparation stage of the creative process tune our ears toward hearing the frequency of God's creative energy at work in our lives. Listening below the surface of events, we hear the undercurrent that is the heartbeat of God. Through prayer the pilgrim learns to listen the way the artist listens—with the whole heart.

The creative process and the pilgrim's journey are not for the cowardly. Both call for courage to remain open to the unexpected. God and creativity come in mysterious and frequently unanticipated ways. Without a willingness to keep the heart open, we cannot receive new insights in the creative process; neither can we receive new revelations from God. Listening well, with our whole heart, keeps both creativity and faith alive and vital. It propels the artist and the pilgrim into a dynamic process that perpetuates life in all its goodness.

Exercise

Listening for the Whole Notes

> *Listen to your life. See it for the fathomless mystery
> that it is. In the boredom and pain of it no less than
> in the excitement and gladness: touch, taste, smell
> your way to the holy and hidden heart of it because
> in the last analysis all moments are key moments,
> and life itself is grace.*
>
> —FREDERICK BUECHNER[6]

MATERIALS NEEDED
> *several pieces of poster paper or 18" x 24" drawing paper*
> *a variety of your favorite music*
> *container of water*
> *paint rag*
> *watercolors or tempera paints*
> *paintbrush*

How would life be different if you knew how to listen better? What would you hear if you were listening to your own desires? to the voice of God within? to the cries of the world? Listening is a basic spiritual discipline, one with which everyone needs help.

In this exercise you are going to practice listening. Get out your paints and put on some music. Poster-size paper is the best, but any kind will do, even paper grocery bags. You may want to experiment with different kinds of music. Try this exercise with an instrumental piece first; sometimes words get in the way of our hearing.

This quick exercise primes the pump of the creative well. Use it whenever you get ready to paint from the soul. Try to complete your painting in the time it takes for one song to play. Keep the painting loose. You are not painting a picture as much as you are limbering up your listening and creativity.

As the music begins, paint the emotions of the song. What is the song communicating? Listen to the notes and endeavor to paint them. Go for the feeling of the song. Be attentive to the color choices the music provokes within you. Close your eyes and paint to the beat.

Repeat the exercise with various musical selections. When you have completed two or three different paintings, compare and contrast the experiences. What have you learned about listening? Has painting the music helped you to hear?

Traveling Alone

The Lord answered her, "Martha, Martha, you are worried and distracted by many things; there is need of only one thing. Mary has chosen the better part, which will not be taken away from her."

—LUKE 10:41-42

Every time I face a fresh canvas or a blank sheet of paper, I fear I have nothing to say. It is not just a little fear—as in, "I'm afraid it's going to rain today and I might need an umbrella." It is a big one—as in, "I'll never be able to leap the Grand Canyon even from a running start, and I know I must find a way." I feel enormously inadequate to the task. This fear leads me to all kinds of well-honed procrastinating behaviors. I clean the kitchen or the closet, walk the dog, make phone calls, eat a snack. I decide I must exercise, grocery shop, or write thank you notes—anything to avoid feeling I have nothing to say. Eventually tiring of those avoidance behaviors, I reach the point when I must commit to the creative process because doing so causes less pain than continuing to procrastinate. I dive headfirst into a process that inevitably will take me where I did not plan on going. In deciding to commit, I make a leap of faith into the unknown—an act of total trust that at the end of the process a work of art will have manifested itself in some coherent form and shape. It is every bit as much a leap of faith as the pilgrim's yes to God's call and willingness to go wherever God leads.

My avoidance behaviors camouflage a deeper fear below the surface. Art is and always will be to some degree about self-expression. It has the power to reveal us to ourselves. As artists we do not always like what we see mirrored in our creations. I sometimes feel like I am standing naked before an audience of hundreds or standing naked before God. I would like to grab a fig leaf or two, but to do so would lessen the creative outcome.

INTO THE INNER LIFE

The decision to begin the creative process commits us to an exploration of the inner life. The discoveries made there merit our whole attention and all our compassion. The journey inward reveals our gifts and our graces—who we truly are and were always meant to be. However, the move inward also risks uncovering wounds and fears, revealing how they have distorted our true identity. The journey inward leads the artist and the pilgrim to relinquish whatever masks or hinders the true self. Just as Martha did not understand Mary's choice to sit at the feet of Jesus, our families and friends may not understand or support the arduous journey we choose.

The Jewish philosopher Philo of Alexandria is credited with saying, "Be kind. Everyone you meet is fighting a great battle." That wisdom not only offers good advice about how to treat others but also provides excellent counsel about how to treat yourself when you commit to traveling inward. Be kind to yourself. While it may feel at times as if you are fighting a great battle, the effort is worthwhile. Though difficult, the journey leads to a place of deep peace.

A Solitary Journey

This inward journey is by necessity a solitary one. We must travel alone the narrow path into the solitude of our own heart. There we find the healing we seek. Artists have an advantage when it comes to solitude. Because so much of creativity requires a degree of physical solitude, artists must come to terms with it as an integral part of their call. Being alone often acts as a catalyst for developing inner solitude.

Inner solitude is a way of life. I may be physically alone yet have no solitude, just as I may be in the middle of a bustling city experiencing a rich, interior solitude. Inner solitude invites us to live from the place where our true identity is enveloped in the peace of Christ. This solitude anchors us in the midst of life's tribulations. When we are surrounded by chaos, the experience of solitude allows us to stand firmly on solid ground. It holds our focus on the one thing needful in the midst of all that competes for our attention. Without inner solitude, life ceases to have meaning as we are tossed to and fro by the whims of the world.

An inescapable component of the spiritual journey, solitude does not require every pilgrim to lead an austere monastic existence. It does, however, compel us as pilgrims to find a way into the still point at the center of our being where the deep peace of Christ resides. Befriending solitude may call for periodically setting time and space apart from the crowd and business of life.

Henri Nouwen, in *The Way of the Heart*, writes, "Solitude is the furnace of transformation. Without solitude we remain victims of our society and continue to be entangled in the illusions of the false self."[7] Inner solitude has the potential to uncover who we are and to Whom we belong. Solitude exposes us to ourselves so that we may discover how God sees us. All the external identities that we have allowed to define us are stripped away. The identities our friends and families give us through their expectations and the roles we play vanish in the solitude of the heart. The celebrity enjoyed from memberships in clubs and organizations and the titles and accomplishments acquired mean nothing in the face of inner solitude. Many will be tempted to avoid the discipline of solitude because of its revealing and transforming nature; however, it divulges the only life worth living.

A Matter of Life and Death

The early church fathers and mothers felt that solitude was a matter of life and death. They fled from the cities into the desert where they could peel off their external identities in the barren wilderness. In the ensuing solitude of the heart they found abundant life. The desert abbas and ammas wanted to be defined only by God, so they escaped to the lonely wilderness seeking their true identity in Christ. In the desert, with few outer distractions competing for their attention, the abbas and ammas concentrated fully on their inner life. They allowed their external identities to die, only to wrestle with their inner habits of greed, lust, jealousy, and laziness—all those characteristics that got in the way of who they were meant to be. They worked at relinquishing their bad habits and unloving thoughts so they could put on the mind and heart of Christ.

When Christ calls the pilgrim, it is to leave behind the false self and all untrue identities in the way the desert mothers and fathers left the cities. Christ invites us as pilgrims to relinquish those habits, attitudes, beliefs, expectations, and wounds that keep us from being who we truly are. Just as the rich young ruler was asked to relinquish his wealth, we are asked to die to our false self so that our true self might be born. Sometimes dying to the false self requires an enormous physical change, such as a move or a new job, but most often the changes will be small and internal, like developing inner solitude. No one will realize we are making changes until one day we seem kinder, gentler, and more compassionate.

When creativity calls the artist, it is to commit to the creative process, to leap across the Grand Canyon of fear, trusting in a safe landing. Whether we are pilgrims or artists, saying yes to the invitation of a solitary journey inward is to strip off external identities and to let that process take us wherever it leads—even into battle with our demons.

Exercise

Excess Baggage

Two roads diverged in a wood, and I—
I took the one less traveled by

—ROBERT FROST[8]

MATERIALS NEEDED
18" x 24" drawing paper
colored markers
tempera paints
paintbrush
container for water
paint rag

I first began to develop inner solitude on the pilgrim's journey through centering prayer. Before long I noticed that creating art from the soul took me to a similar place. My biggest difficulty in both disciplines was the distraction of incessant thoughts that agitated me, making it impossible to center down into the solitude and silence. My to-do list would suddenly pop into my head one chore at a time as I sank into the solitude. I learned to imagine a pad of paper and pencil along with a trash basket. With these I mentally disposed of those thoughts, trusting I could retrieve them whenever I chose to do so. I seldom found it necessary to recover the thoughts I mentally released. In most cases I was freed to move into the renewing silence through this simple imaginary gesture.

Ask the One Who Meets Us in the silence to guide you through this time. As you begin to move into silence and solitude, notice your thoughts and write them on the paper with markers or pencils. Every time you have a thought, write it on the paper, no matter what the thought is. Then return to the silence. After what feels like a reasonable time, put the writing utensils aside and get out the paints. Begin to paint on the same sheet of paper on which you have just written. If it seems appropriate, paint over your written thoughts. Block out the words entirely or incorporate them into the painting. They can be part of the design. Remember you do not need to create realistic images. Use only the colors to which you are drawn.

When finished, reflect on this exercise. What did it feel like to write out your thoughts? What did you notice when you blocked out the written thoughts with color or incorporated them into the design of the painting?

Give thanks for whatever you have learned.

Smell the Roses

So do not worry about tomorrow, for tomorrow will bring worries of its own. Today's trouble is enough for today.

—Matthew 6:34

Buddhist monk and Vietnamese poet Thich Nhat Hanh was visiting a midwestern university in the sixties. While waiting for elevator doors to open, Thich Nhat Hanh looked at the electric clock above those doors. Turning to his companion, author Jim Forest, he said, "You know, Jim, a few hundred years ago it would not have been a clock; it would have been a crucifix."[9]

Time has more power and control over our lives than most religious symbols; it has become our idol and our enemy. In a culture that is too much in a hurry, the preparation phase of the creative process often involves slowing down both physically and mentally. Our Western minds race at such an intense pace that the mere thought of being creative feels like a chore rather than a blessing. Our lives are overstructured and overstimulated, our bodies stressed by the inhumane schedules we keep. If inspiration did break through the flurry of activity around and within us, we wouldn't recognize it. Perceived as just one more burden on our tyrannical to-do list, inspiration takes a backseat to frenetic activity. Creativity requires time. Like communing with God, it cannot be hurried or forced.

The Invitation of Creativity and Prayer

As an artist, before I can move into the painstakingly slow work of creativity, I need to step off the treadmill. I am not able to create at one-hour intervals in the middle of a heavily scheduled day. As a pilgrim, I cannot sink into the depth of prayer when I feel the constraints of time. I need space and time to create and to pray, but slowing down is not easy. Stepping off the treadmill once life reaches a certain momentum proves difficult because we receive little cultural support. We go against the norm of our society when we stop to smell the roses. However, creativity and prayer invite us to do just that.

A Culture in a Hurry

Our left-brain-dominant culture, always in a hurry, perpetuates the modern perception of insufficient time. Instead of living in sync with nature's slower rhythms, we measure time in minutes and seconds, burning the midnight oil rather than sleeping under the light of the moon. We worry things will fall apart should we slow down. Lying in bed at night unable to turn off our thoughts, we believe much depends on us. What will become of all the projects if they aren't finished? What will people think if we can't accomplish all our work? What will we think of ourselves? When we fall behind, the pressure in our lives intensifies. Fearing we won't be ready for what lies ahead, we speed up our days, trying to complete one more task before falling exhausted into bed too tired to dream. When our fears and anxieties drive us, the speed of our days only increases as the meaning of our days diminishes.

By hurrying, we get ahead of ourselves and begin to live into the worries and "what ifs" of tomorrow. However, the here and now remains all we have with which to make something beautiful of our life for God. Each sterling moment presents the raw material of our days. If we miss the present moment by rushing through the day, we cannot recapture it. The gift of each day is often squandered in a hurry.

Time management as a spiritual issue speaks to the condition of the soul, and the soul of the Western world needs healing. Even when numerous demands require our time, we need to slow down and enjoy life's pleasures, to treat time as a sacred creation rather than a commodity to be used up. Slowing down allows us to experience the subtle but deeper nuances of life that give it meaning. Compare the experiences of walking through a forest and speeding by the same forest in a car. On a walk you notice more, and noticing is an initial component of contemplative prayer.

UNFETTERED TIME

Our best hope for curing a runaway mind and a runaway heart may be creativity and contemplative prayer. Because they both require unhurried time, making space for these activities in our life may restore a simpler pace and give meaning to our existence. Any spiritual pilgrim who has practiced contemplative prayer for a long time knows its power to free us from the grip of workaholism. Contemplative prayer allows us to be with God without doing anything and without striving. Resting in Divine Presence, we experience the truth of our being. Life is a gift. We are God's beloved. No matter what we do, we cannot earn our life or God's love.

Regular contemplative prayer teaches us to cease our busyness, do nothing, and feel no guilt. It shows us that God guides all our activities, even rest. Contemplative prayer, practiced regularly, discloses the truth hidden in our self-reliance; we are not autonomous but dependent upon God for our every breath. These revelations release us from anxious striving and allow us to step out of the rat race.

Artists faithful to the creative process know the importance of being unfettered by the pressure of time. Every artist engages the right hemisphere of the brain to create. The activity of this hemisphere permits us to be imaginative, to dream, and to understand metaphors. The right side of the brain is free of time constraints. Because so much of creativity employs the right brain, artists are regarded as free spirits precisely because they are less consumed by the power of the clock than other segments of society.

The creative process follows no set schedule. Some artists may awaken in the middle of the night inspired with new insight, work until dawn, and sleep the morning away. Others may show up in the studio every morning at eight o'clock for a week and have only one good day of work to show for it. No matter how much the artist wants to accomplish in any given day, the creative process remains in charge of the "when." The artist, whose job is to be present to the creative process, cannot be attentive when overscheduled and suffering from time shortage.

When working on a creative project, I practice opening up space in my calendar. Timidly, at first, I look at my calendar with God as if I am packing for a long trip. I don't want to carry any more weight than absolutely necessary. After several passes through the weeks, I develop a ruthless eye, intent on making time for something immensely precious. I cancel all appointments and activities that are not a matter of survival. I draw a dark line through all the blank spaces as a reminder not to schedule any unnecessary appointments. For my true self—the artist pilgrim within me—to survive I must have unhurried and unworried time in which to create.

THE GIFT

In *The Tao of Pooh*, Benjamin Hoff tells about an incident in the life of the Japanese emperor Hirohito. The emperor lived an extremely busy existence. From sunup to sundown a tight schedule of meetings, speeches, audiences, and other important duties dictated his movements. One busy day, there was a colossal foul-up in the scheduling. The emperor was driven to a huge meeting hall where he was to address a group. When he arrived, he found the hall empty.

The emperor walked into the middle of the large room, stood silently for several moments, then bowed to the empty space. With a large smile on his face, he turned to his assistant and said, "We must schedule more appointments like this. I haven't enjoyed myself so much in a long time."[10]

Slowing down fosters the enjoyment of time as a gift from the Holy One. It imbues our moments with quality and enriches our experiences. Each hour well lived enables the artist and the pilgrim to make meaning of their days.

Exercise

Making Room for God

*God, whose name is love, offers us—with every
breath we take—a new, transforming energy for our
tense, stress-filled bodies and an inner healing that
reaches depths we had not dreamed!*

—FLORA WUELLNER[11]

MATERIALS NEEDED
breath

When our lives are too full, we have no room for God.
Sometimes a spiritual spring-cleaning can restore order to
our busyness by clearing room for the Holy One. When I do
spring-cleaning, I tackle one room at a time, a manageable
approach for me. The key to cleaning the entire house is to set
small, realistic goals. The same approach applies to the spiritual life: we shouldn't bite off more than we can chew. We
begin slowly and build on our practices.

This exercise will help you take the first step toward making room for God. Take a few minutes to focus awareness on
your breath. Working with the breath offers the simplest way
to slow yourself down. When you focus on the breath, you give
attention to the way God moves in your life. *Breath* and *spirit*
are the same word in many ancient languages: in Hebrew,
ruach; in Greek, *pneuma*; in Latin, *spiritus*. God has chosen to
transform the world through flesh and blood like an artist
working in a medium. Using creative energy God breathes
beauty into people. The simple act of mindful breathing can
make space in busy lives for God to work.

Inhaling deeply through the nose and exhaling through the mouth will help the rest of the body to relax. As you exhale, make an audible noise as if blowing out a candle. When you inhale, think the word *Christ, God,* or *Spirit,* as if you are inhaling the very presence of Love. When you exhale, imagine letting go of anything you no longer need. After several deep breaths, allow your breath to return to a normal resting state, remaining consciously focused upon it. If you have not begun to sense you are sinking into a more relaxed state, return to deep breathing, followed by a normal resting breath. Stay with the breathing exercise for a few moments until you are in a receptive and calm state of being.

Frustration

Essential Frustration—
and God's New Thing

I am about to do a new thing;
now it springs forth, do you not perceive it?

—ISAIAH 43:19

Artists experience frustration on a regular basis because it is the third stage of the creative process. Every time an artist begins a new project, confusion and chaos are built into it. The resulting frustration, this natural ingredient of creativity, comes from sorting through numerous possibilities for the best solution to the current creative challenge. It acts as the grain of sand in the oyster from which the pearl of an idea manifests. Though frequently less than fun, without frustration, there would be no art.

No matter how many creative projects I undertake, the frustration stage still takes me by surprise. I erroneously expect creativity to be smooth and effortless. Associating frustration with lack of talent, I tell myself, *If I were really gifted I wouldn't feel this frustrated.* This faulty reasoning resembles the spiritual pilgrim's mistaken belief that *good Christians never get angry or feel upset by the challenges of life.* Nonsense! Emotions—for the artist and the spiritual pilgrim—simply come with being human. They have nothing to do with how much talent we have or how faithful we are. Emotions provide grist for the mill, tools for our growth. The problem develops when an emotion overtakes us, and we get stuck in it.

Hiding in the Belly of a Fish

Each time I come to this phase of the creative process, I am tempted, if only briefly, to give up. I want to run from frustration like Jonah ran from Nineveh—full speed in the opposite direction. However, I cannot escape my call. I can stall the creative process for a while and frequently do. Like Jonah hiding out in the belly of a fish for three days, I hide out by pretending the project has no importance for me. Other legitimate needs in my life take on exaggerated urgency. Usually it is not the trivial things that stall the process but good and well-intentioned stuff—like my mission the day after our dog encountered a skunk.

We were expecting a houseguest one evening when I was feeling frustrated with a writing project. All the ideas and words in my head seemed jumbled in one chaotic mess. Nothing I wrote made sense. It suddenly became imperative that I remove the faint but lingering traces of skunk scent off the dog and out of the guest bathtub where my dutiful spouse had bathed the dog numerous times. My husband had scoured the tub in an attempt to eliminate the odor, but the scent of skunk hung on. Like a Stepford wife, I found myself scrubbing the bathtub at four different intervals on the day we expected the houseguest. I interspersed the cleaning with Internet research on removal of skunk odor. While a clean-smelling bathroom is more hospitable than one that smells bad, it is also true that we had another bathroom available for guests. The more frustrated I became with my writing, the more critical it became to have a bathtub free from the almost-imperceptible traces of skunk odor.

Abandoning the Process

The frustration stage of the creative process causes many artists to abandon creativity altogether in order to avoid the discomfort accompanying this phase. The painting remains undone because emotions get in the way; agitation keeps the great ideas and good intentions from ever coming to fruition. I know an artist who gets all excited over an idea for a new project, seems to proceed at a rapid pace, then runs up against the brick wall of frustration at full speed. That stops him cold. The expectation that creativity should always feel good and be easy is his brick wall. His creative idea dies on impact and so does a little of his artist's spirit, especially since this pattern recurs. If he ever wants to complete a project, he must learn to deal with the frustration that makes him want to throw paint on the wall instead of applying it to canvas.

Forcing a premature conclusion to the creative process also tempts the artist who dislikes frustration. Watching a friend create, I am struck by how her process develops. Her prototype looks good enough to sell; but by going deeper into her creativity, she ends up with a masterpiece. The prototype now looks like a shadow of the completed work. Sometimes in my work, I'd like to settle for the prototype just so I will not have to plumb the depths of the creative process. Getting to the marrow of the initial inspiration requires hard and lonely work. But, like a person committed to a cause, I press on because to force a premature conclusion to the creative process fails to let the work of art be all it can be.

When tempted to run like Jonah, I remind myself that frustration is not just a stage to endure, although sometimes a tenacious endurance may be our best effort. As childbirth requires labor pains, creativity necessitates frustration as part of the process. It causes the artist to go deeper into the source of creativity, bringing forth new life and energy previously known only in the imagination. Once the labor pains of creativity have begun, the only way out of the frustration—without aborting the creative idea—leads straight through it. Out of chaos comes brilliance and beauty if the artist will stay with the process.

RESTLESSNESS ON THE JOURNEY

The faith journey also includes periods of frustration and aridity. We seldom talk about these times, preferring to focus on the good feelings of the faith journey. But to grow in our ability to love God, neighbor, and ourselves, eventually we will experience some feelings of discomfort. Though unpleasant, frustration with the inner life can signal important change for the spiritual pilgrim.

Restlessness, the mildest form of frustration, occurs when we feel slightly unsettled. Life seems a little out of kilter. Maybe we have outgrown a job, a relationship, or our living space. We may have become complacent in our prayer life or feel a lack we cannot even name. Our days are void of inspiration. Nothing is wrong, but nothing is right either. The presence of restlessness and frustration may be the stirring of the Holy Spirit, informing us something in our life has struck a dissonant chord with God's yearning for us.

A person who came to me for spiritual direction had grown weary with her job; it was draining the life out of her. Although she was doing good, creative work, it was not the work God was calling her to do. As God's voice grew deafening, she quit her job, became self-employed, and now does work that fills her up even as she gives herself to the world.

If an extended case of the blahs does not go away, God may be inviting us to break camp and journey onward. A door may be about to open, one we would not have noticed unless we were looking; and we would not have been looking unless we were restless. Perhaps the Divine has a new kind of work for us. Though our current endeavors remain admirable and worthwhile, they may not be congruent with God's desire for our life. Feelings of distress—whether mild or more severe—may signal the need to travel inward and delve into the source of the discomfort. It may be necessary to find a good spiritual director or counselor to assist with the exploration, especially if the discomfort is severe. Seeking the help of someone who has traversed the inner road can prevent unnecessary pitfalls and make the journey a little easier.

If frustration emerges on the pilgrim's path, especially when we pray, God may be doing a new thing in our prayer life. Where once prayer resulted in peace and joy, it may now feel dry—as if we are only talking to ourselves. For an entire year I was unable to pray as I had been accustomed to praying for eleven years. One day centering prayer simply stopped working for me. Nothing happened when I sat down to enter into the silence. I could not bear the thought of giving up this discipline, but God led me to do just that. Through trial and error, I discovered how to walk and pray. As long as my body was moving, the praying worked. I was communing with God and not just talking to myself. For one year, I used a walking meditation as spiritual sustenance. One day, just as quickly as it had disappeared, the nourishment through centering prayer mysteriously returned.

MOVING CLOSER TO LOVE

When good spiritual feelings dry up, God may be beckoning us closer, into a more intimate relationship with the Source of All Love. In the spiritual life, the false self wants to take credit for any spiritual growth or good feeling. Our false self likes us to believe we—not God—initiate spiritual consolations. Sometimes the Holy One causes the good spiritual feelings to which we have grown accustomed and attached to evaporate. The ensuing sense of aridity prompts us to look beyond those feelings to the true source—to God the Great Gift-giver. This period of spiritual desolation actually invites us to know God more fully. Like the artist who experiences frustration in the creative process, tenacity provides a key for the pilgrim in the midst of a spiritual drought. The Divine Guide will lead the way through dryness just as surely as God led the Hebrew people through the desert to the Promised Land.

As an artist I have observed over time how I deal with frustration. Methods of avoidance cause more discomfort than continuously staying with the creative process. The gnawing in my soul cannot be filled with escape tactics for the artist or the pilgrim within me. My inner artist, who has surrendered again and again to the creative process, has taught my prodigal pilgrim-self to return to the journey no matter how difficult and no matter how often I stray. Every time I come back to the journey, I learn that our Creator God offers unlimited chances to return to the inner path. The Holy One meets us each time we surrender, each time we turn to stare squarely into the face of frustration, confusion, and chaos.

Exercise

Paint Your Heart Out

> One must still have chaos in oneself to be able to give
> birth to a dancing star.
>
> —FRIEDRICH NIETZSCHE[1]

MATERIALS NEEDED
> *two sheets of 18" x 24" drawing paper*
> *tempera paints or watercolors*
> *paintbrush*
> *container for water*
> *paint rag*

Whenever a creative project frustrates me, I get my body moving. I go for a walk, dance to music, or do aerobic exercises. When my spiritual life frustrates me, I walk. Like Forrest Gump, who ran from one end of the country to the other until one day he just stopped running, I walk until I feel better or run out of time. If it is raining or for some other reason I cannot walk, I make art from the soul. It helps ease the frustration just the way walking does.

Before you begin, prayerfully ask the Divine Comforter to be present, guiding you through this exercise. Make sure to allow enough time to do two paintings in one session. You are going to paint a picture of the emotion of frustration. If this feels too difficult, paint your current feelings. Be gentle; do not force yourself.

Remember a time in the past when you were frustrated. It may be recent or long ago, a big frustration or just a minor irritation. Try to remember as many details of the situation as possible, especially how you felt. Using your nondominant hand, dip your paintbrush in a color that attracts you. Begin to move the brush on the paper and listen to your inner voice directing where it belongs. Don't worry about making a realistic representation. Simply move the colors on the paper in a way that feels right to you. It will be impossible to make any mistakes; whatever you do will be okay. Keep painting until you sense you are finished.

Begin a second painting. If frustration remains from the first painting exercise, keep painting until the emotion lessens in intensity. If the first painting has cleared the emotion, paint from the soul in any manner you wish.

When finished, look at your paintings from various angles. Turn them upside down and sideways. What do they reveal to you? Are you surprised by anything? Are there images or partial images you did not intend to paint? If so, how do you interpret these? How did it feel to give expression to your remembering? How do the two paintings compare and contrast? What was it like to do two paintings in a row? What did you learn about yourself?

Give your paintings titles.

Dark Nights and Deserts

How long, O LORD? Will you forget me forever?
How long will you hide your face from me?
How long must I bear pain in my soul,
and have sorrow in my heart all day long?

—PSALM 13:1-2

The frustration stage of the creative process frequently lasts longer than desired. Hoping for an insight to illuminate the way, an artist may have the sense of trying to force a blessing from a reluctant God. Like Jacob wrestling with the stranger in the dark at Peniel, the artist grapples with the creative process in the darkness of confusion and uncertainty. Just as Jacob did not receive the name of his opponent in the darkness of the night, neither does the artist receive a solution to the creative challenge while in the cloud of frustration.

CREATIVE BLOCKS

If this stage of the creative process persists, the artist may fear being stuck in a desert agonizingly barren of ideas. Authors call an extended stay in this arid wilderness writer's block, and artists experience it as purgatory. Any artist who has ever experienced blocked creativity knows this as an excruciating eternity. Waiting for creativity to return produces anxiety and much soul searching.

During a creative drought, written words sound garbled and senseless; painted images look flat and uninspired. Down deep, the artist may wonder if this suffering results from some unidentified sin, which now must be atoned. Those who have traveled this desert wasteland wonder, *What did I do wrong and will I ever have another creative idea again?*

In the desert some things have to die for others to be born. This is my Protestant understanding of what happens in purgatory: sin dies so the soul can be born to eternal life. The artist enduring a creative block experiences a kind of death. If it is the death of a sin, then surely it is the sin of self-doubt that dies in order for creativity to be born.

Being Empty

During a creative block, artists need not fear that a fatal flaw within causes the lack of creativity, but many of us do. We worry and obsess and try to figure out what we have done to deserve such a fate. If we just knew what it was, we would promise never to do it again. If artists experience creative blocks often enough, it may occur to us we are not to blame.

A creative block is not so much about being stuck or stymied as it is about being empty. It comes from spending creativity without replenishing it; much like working all day without eating or sleeping. Sooner or later a person learns eating and sleeping sustain one's work. For artists, recharging the creative batteries is as essential as food and a good night's rest. Blocked artists are actually empty and must take time to fill up the tank with creative juices in order to create again. Artists need to do whatever generates inspiration: take a walk in nature, listen to music, go to a movie, read a book, or make chocolate truffles. Above all else, during a creative block, artists need to silence the voice of self-doubt. Creativity will return once the artist is fully inspired again. It has taken me half a century to learn I cannot create out of nothingness; only God can do that. In order to be creative, I must have a full tank of creative juice.

BEING EMPTIED OUT

A pilgrim may encounter many dry times on the spiritual path, but a prolonged desert experience takes on a unique quality. Such an experience is called the dark night of the soul. If the artist's creative block is about being empty, the pilgrim's dark night is about being emptied out. The dark night may feel like the artist's purgatory, but it is really a purgation. From the root word "to purge," *purgation* hollows out of the pilgrim all that separates the person from the Divine Lover. The Holy One works under the cover of darkness to free the pilgrim from the tyranny of the false self. This purging can feel even more excruciating than the artist's creative block and frequently lasts much longer. Rather than days or weeks, the dark night may continue over months or years.

The dark night can be initiated by events or circumstances in life that throw us against the brick wall: the death of a spouse or family member, divorce, physical or emotional trauma. We may feel as if our skin is being turned inside out, and we are helpless to do anything about it. However, a dark night does not always commence with a tragedy. It may emerge out of the blue as life clips along at a decent pace. Our daily tasks suddenly become meaningless. Everything we thought we desired holds no luster; even our goals appear unimportant. And God seems incredibly distant.

While vacationing with my family one summer I stepped into a dark night of the soul. Everything was going well in my life. I enjoyed fulfilling work, a good family, and a wonderfully supportive community, but I was restless and wondering if I needed a change. I started to feel odd, as if something was different with me, but I could not put my finger on it. A pervasive fear seeped into my cells and engulfed me. For the first time in my life I felt as if God had vacated the premises. Even in dry periods on my journey, I had sensed the Ground of My Being present with me. This was different. God was not merely silent but apparently had gone on vacation too. I searched my soul to see if I had caused this change. Did I need to recommit my life to Christ? How could I get God to come back? Reading the Bible seemed nearly impossible. I did not want to think about God; I wanted to experience God. The only piece of scripture that made any sense to me was Romans 8:38-39, which tells us "nothing can separate us from the love of God." I desperately wanted to believe it but no longer knew if it were true. I felt abandoned by God and cut off from the Source of divine love; this awareness shook me to my core.

THREE SIGNS OF THE DARK NIGHT

Saint John of the Cross, the sixteenth-century Spanish mystic, describes three signs that denote the dark night of the soul. Without all three, the lack of energy for life may in fact be depression, the result of sin, or another psychological or physical difficulty.

The first sign is dryness in our prayer life and everyday life. The ease and good feelings previously present in our prayer life vanish. Without gratification, our prayers seem empty, and so does the rest of our life. Relationships, work, and leisure activities that used to bring us joy now feel like chores. Nothing we do seems to improve our state of being. Even new activities and relationships that hold out a promise of respite from the soul-wrenching aridity evaporate like a desert mirage once we get close enough to see them clearly. Satisfaction in any area of life appears unattainable; everything feels flat.

The second telltale sign of a dark night is losing desire to live and pray the way we used to pray and live. This sign feels disturbingly similar to apathy. Our old way of life no longer appeals to us. Any attempts to carry on life as usual stem not from desire but from duty. Fearful of backsliding on our faith journey, we wonder if we have blown it with God. The self-doubt present in the artist's creative block shows itself here to the pilgrim. We may think we are to blame for the absence of spiritual consolations and that it is our fault life has gone awry. Searching our souls to figure out where God went and why, we may even feel betrayed by our Maker.

We sense God's abandonment; however, unbeknownst to us, the Holy One is very present, putting in place yet unfamiliar ways of knowing divine love. Though we might be tempted to believe God withholds those good spiritual feelings out of punishment, in the dark night the Divine actually teaches us to let go of our reliance on them. Formerly, we experienced God through our senses and our reasoning; now we are being taught to rely on faith to know God. We may think we have erred on the pilgrim's path; however, the truth is, we have done something right. The dark night of the soul occurs only when pilgrims are serious about the inner journey.

The final sign of the dark night of the soul is a simple desire to be alone with God. Even with this desire to love and serve God, there remains an inability to know how to proceed. We perceive that we cannot concentrate on exercises of prayer;

religion may leave us cold; and we have no desire to think about God at all. Yet a deep yearning to be alone with the Source of Love and to soak up Love's presence persists.

Even though our desire for God appears unrequited, nothing could be further from the truth. The Divine is so incredibly in love with us; God pours God's very self into our soul. Ironically, in the holy darkness God infuses us with more light. The very presence of Love works under the cover of darkness until we embody more of that Love. Love cleanses and illuminates the pilgrim's soul. The unconscious motivations of the false self come to light and are transformed. As we are freed from the false self, our desire to look for love and happiness in all the wrong places lessens. In the returning dawn, we seek and find our happiness in God alone.

EMPTY HANDS

The dark night of the soul can last for months or years. We cannot quickly negotiate a clear path through it. Ten months after my dark night began, I became aware of it slowly lifting. Like a butterfly emerging from its cocoon, I was not ready to fly, but I could smell the fresh air.

A small, carved female figure came into my possession a year after the onset of my dark night. This beautiful dark-skinned woman stands erect with open and empty hands. I treasure her because she symbolizes my experience of the refining dark night. Whatever I had held on to in my faith before the dark night was gone; my hands had been pried open and emptied out. The dark night instilled within the marrow of my bones the wisdom that God was holding me and will always hold me. Under the cover of darkness, in ways I can never understand, I was freed from the illusion that I am capable of holding on to God. Mercifully and tenderly, God does the holding, and all I can do is say yes.

The desert experiences of the artist and the pilgrim leave us limping like Jacob into the dawn of a new day. Having survived the struggle, we now realize the blessing: we are not in control of either the creative process or the faith journey. This knowledge grants the artist an ability to relinquish hold on the creative process, opening up greater depths of creativity. It releases the pilgrim from misguided attempts to find happiness outside the love and mercy of God. The pilgrim, stripped of the false self and the illusion of control, now recognizes the infinite futility of such a search. These blessings bring a new dimension of humility. With hands humbly opened, the artist and the pilgrim receive the gifts of creativity and joy.

Exercise

Holy Darkness

In our sleep, pain that cannot forget
falls drop by drop
upon the heart and in our despair,
against our will comes
wisdom through the awful grace of God.

—AESCHYLUS[2]

MATERIALS NEEDED
18" x 24" drawing paper
tempera paints or watercolors
paintbrush
container for water
paint rag
journal and pen

For most pilgrims, the dark night eventually passes, but in the midst of the dark night, we feel as if our survival depends on endurance. During my dark night, it was crucial to have the prayers of others for support. Making art from the soul can be helpful too.

Before beginning this exercise, prayerfully ask the One Who Never Leaves Us to guide you. Even if you feel no presence, trust that the Spirit surrounds you in love. Take your time. If at any point you feel you cannot proceed, do not force yourself. The One Who Never Leaves Us will guide you lovingly at a pace suited to your needs.

Ask God to lead you in identifying an experience of dryness or a dark night of the soul from past or present circumstance. Paint this experience. Remember your painting does not have to look realistic; you may paint a representation of pure emotion. The painting may or may not depict recognizable objects. The point of the painting is listening to the still small voice while remaining faithful to the creative process. Allow the creativity to take you where it wants to go.

Stay with the painting until you sense completion. When you finish, write about your experience on a blank piece of paper or in your journal. Try to remain nonjudgmental toward yourself and your experience.

How did you survive the dry period in your life? What coping mechanisms did you use? Which ones worked? Which coping mechanisms were not helpful? What ways of dealing with aridity would you like to try in the future should you need them? Make a list.

Demons and Passions

Be merciful to me, O God, be merciful to me,
for in you my soul takes refuge;
in the shadow of your wings I will take refuge,
until the destroying storms pass by.

—PSALM 57:1

The insidious demon of perfectionism can frustrate the artist at any and all stages of the creative process. Though frustration emerges as a natural effect of the preparation stage, frustration resulting from perfectionism differs in character. Perfectionism can delay the beginning of any creative project or stop us in our tracks halfway through. As the harsh voice of criticism within, it says, *Don't even bother; you won't get it right.* Perfectionism tells us what we do is never, ever good enough. It holds the power to kill many good ideas and many artists' spirit.

This demon has prevented me from painting for years at a time; it is one of my biggest hurdles as an artist. The need for perfection has clogged up my creative flow like a logjam, funneling my creativity into everything but my preferred medium. Perfectionism has caused me to entomb half-finished canvases in my closets like skeletons waiting for embodiment. For years I believed that what I created must look like a da Vinci masterpiece or read like a Shakespearean sonnet. The demon of perfectionism left no room for a learning curve; no rough sketches or first drafts were allowed. A project had to be perfect from the start.

The Many Faces of Perfectionism

A master of disguise, perfectionism showed itself to me in many forms. It appeared as procrastination—delaying the start of numerous projects over the years and causing heightened anxiety over looming deadlines. This cagey, seductive shape shifter even materialized as a self-righteous judge of other artists' work. I cannot count the times I have looked at another artist's work and coldly criticized it for not being good enough. I told myself, *I could have done that and done it better.* But I did not do better; in fact, I did not do anything at all. Judging another's work came easier than creating art myself.

Perfectionists need the reaction of others in order to form an identity. Without another's opinion we don't know who we are. This attitude robs an artist of the freedom to create without concern for what others might think. Since art grows out of self-expression, creating with concern for public approval pollutes the process. How can art be self-expression if the artist focuses on getting a reaction from others?

The demon of perfectionism can make the artist a people pleaser. Needing to have the public's approval keeps the artist looking outside himself or herself for an identity. No one ever finds it there. Perfectionistic, people-pleasing artists may seem to know who they are at one moment; but if the scenery changes, their search for identity begins all over again. An externally referenced identity produces wishy-washy, chameleon-like artists. Until external praise or insult have no effect, the artist will not be free from the demon.

Ironically, the demon called perfectionism may appear in the guise of being stuck in the victim's role. This posture also keeps the artist focused outward in search of an identity. The victim-artist blames others for failure. "It's all my parents' fault that I'm not a successful artist." "If that art dealer had more taste, she'd be selling my work." "If my family didn't need me so much, I'd have more time to paint [or write, dance, etc.]."

Blaming others rather than taking responsibility for mistakes and shortcomings allows the artist to stay hidden behind the shadow of the false self. Seemingly easier than making the changes necessary to allow the true self to emerge, blaming keeps the victim-artist from experiencing the much-desired creative life.

More subtle than blame, using others as an excuse not to create permits the artist to be defined by an external source. "My spouse needs me." "The church or neighborhood association needs me." "How will the office ever get along without me?" "My music isn't so important; other people have more pressing needs than mine." The end result stays the same. Artists in the victim's role give away their creative self one piece at a time and never figure out who they truly are. Perfectionism in all its guises is a ploy of the false self that keeps the artist from moving closer to authentic identity found in the heart of God.

The Passions

The ancient monastics identified perfectionism as a passion in the life of the pilgrim. While we moderns associate passion with sexuality and strong emotions, the early monastics did not. For them a passion denoted a negative characteristic that wrecked havoc with love, diminishing the pilgrim's capacity to see it, to accept it, and to give it.

In the spiritual life, passions skew the pilgrim's perception of self, neighbor, and God. Passions can take the form of depression, envy, jealousy, gluttony, pride, timidity, resentment, gossip, or perfectionism—to name a few. These ways of thinking, being, feeling, or acting get in the way of our ability to see and respond to life with love. Our passions tell us we are unimportant, unloved, and unlovable. They make us feel there is not enough love to go around and that we must earn what little love there is. They fool us into seeing others through distorted lenses, turning our sisters and brothers into competitors instead of family. The passions diminish our capacity for life and love. At the root of all the passions is a misunderstanding of God's love.

The monastics used the image of demons to talk about doing battle with the passions. They understood the power of a passion to be similar to the power of addiction. An addiction, such as alcoholism, appears to have power over us; it feels beyond our control. We did not ask for the genetic makeup that sets this disease in motion. Yet we are not entirely helpless against the disease. We can choose to attend Twelve-Step meetings, find a sponsor, and avoid consumption. It is partly the sense that passions are both beyond and within our control that led the monastics to use images of demons to address their power in our lives.

We initially give our consent to passions, but then they begin to consume us, diminish our freedom, and decrease our ability to love. Just as we fail to see the damage addictions do to our lives and those around us, we are blinded by our passions. They keep us living a lie. Passions are the tools of the false self.

In the discipline of solitude and in the desert experience on the spiritual journey, the demons come out in full force, dangling our passions before our eyes. In the desert the effects of our passions are magnified, and we are able to see them clearly. Rather than running from our passions, we have an opportunity to deal with their stranglehold on our life. Dismantling our passions requires courage, love, and a willingness to be honest with ourselves.

HELP FOR THE PASSIONS

Dealing with our passions will not be much fun. We might learn we are not as innately kind to others as we thought or find out we harbor anger at God for making life so difficult. We even may be surprised to recognize the dullness below the surface as depression. In the battle to overcome these demon-passions, whether in the desert or in solitude, it is important to remember not to do this work alone. We cannot do it alone. The only power great enough to defeat the demons in battle is the love of God. Wise pilgrims call upon the help of Christ to face the passions, because facing them without Christ's assistance opens the way for the demons to overpower us.

As an artist-pilgrim who yearns to be free from the stranglehold of perfectionism in my work and in my life, I frequently pray, asking Christ to go before me to fight the battle and prepare the path. I pray, "I can't, but God can." I pray this every day, several times a day when I am confronted with my passions. I do it before I get out of bed, as I sit down to write, before I paint, and upon retiring in the evening. I pray this prayer because to live controlled by a passion is to live only part of the life that wants to be lived in me.

For the artist and the pilgrim, daily confrontations with the passions give ample opportunity to practice surrendering them to God. When picking up a paintbrush, typing the first words of a novel, or playing the introductory notes of a song, the artist surrenders with faith that creativity will come. Faith is necessary for the pilgrim too. In relinquishing passions to God, the pilgrim trusts the promise that every letting go is a step closer to the place of personal resurrection. With each act of creativity and each step of the journey, the artist and the pilgrim pray, "I can't, but God can."

Exercise

Dwelling in the House of Love

> *Hardly a day passes in our lives without our experience of inner or outer fears, anxieties, apprehensions and preoccupations. These dark powers have pervaded every part of our world to such a degree that we can never fully escape them. Still it is possible not to belong to these powers, not to build our dwelling place among them, but to choose the house of love as our home.*
>
> —Henri J. M. Nouwen[3]

MATERIALS NEEDED
> *two sheets of 18" x 24" drawing paper*
> *colored markers*

Some days I am constantly surrendering my anxieties and preoccupations to the Source of Love. I want to live in the house of God's love. The choice is intentional; I make it with the help of daily doses of divine grace. Before I can surrender my passions, I need an awareness of what I am actually surrendering.

This exercise will give you time to examine your own passions. Prayerfully ask the One Who Loves Us to be present, guiding you through the exercise. If at any point you feel you cannot proceed, do not force yourself. God's loving Spirit will direct you according to your needs.

Picture in your mind's eye the Spirit of Love or the Living Christ going before you to guide the way. Ask for help in identifying a passion that keeps you from being creative. Anything that keeps you from being your true self also keeps you from being fully creative. Reflect on the ways this passion inhibits your creativity. When was the last time you felt yourself to be in the throes of this passion?

Using colored markers, draw the effects of this passion in your life. When you finish, reread Henri Nouwen's quote. What does the house of love look like? See if you can picture it in your mind's eye. Now do another drawing that shows you living in "the house of love," free of your passion.

Incubation

Let It Be

*Then Mary said, "Here am I, the servant of the Lord;
let it be with me according to your word."*

—LUKE 1:38

As I stood in the early morning line at my favorite local coffee shop, the familiar Lennon-McCartney song "Let It Be" filled the sleepy silence. One of the baby boomers in front of me sang along with the music in half whispers. As McCartney crooned, "Let it be," the same three words Mary used at the Annunciation, the atmosphere in the coffee shop transformed into sacred space. It felt like church. The lyrics and melody moved me to a place of earnest hope and radical trust. Somehow the song had become a corporate prayer, and those of us in the coffee shop seemed to be asking for the same thing: give us the ability to trust more, to hope more, to live with greater faith.

The truth distilled in the lyrics of the once-popular song describes the incubation stage of the creative process. McCartney sings "there will be an answer" if we let it be, if we trust and wait. If the frustration stage teaches the artist how to surrender, the incubation stage shows the artist how to get out of the way. A period of deliberately doing nothing about the current creative challenge actually gives way to a solution. Like yeasty bread dough rising undisturbed, the work of this stage happens without the artist's conscious attention. It may appear that nothing is happening on the surface, but creative energy ferments in the recesses of the artist's mind and heart, giving rise to new ideas and fresh creativity—if the artist will only get out of the way.

A PRODUCTIVE LIFE

Multitasking is a concept popular among my friends. We share the various ways we combine our chores in order to complete them more quickly. A telephone conversation presents the opportunity to file papers, wash dishes, pay bills, or fold laundry. Making good use of time defines the goal of multitasking. The busier we are, the more productive we consider ourselves. Our cultural need for productivity may explain the increased use of cellular phones. Cell phones allow us to do two things at once: exercise and simultaneously close a business deal, or drive the car while setting up a luncheon date.

Our society looks at productivity as a measuring stick for self-worth. If we are not productive, we judge ourselves not worth much. I feel better after a day of writing if I have something to show for my efforts—words, and lots of them, coherently strung together on a crisp sheet of paper. The days when I delete more words than I've saved or stare blankly at the computer screen make me question my value and wonder if I correctly heard God's call to write. Surely God didn't mean I was to spend hours laboring with nothing to show for my time at the end of the day.

Western society struggles with the concept of incubation. Doing nothing is almost impossible for those of us who believe we are what we produce. The scientific community has taught us if it's not measurable, it's not real. Our factories measure production output, and our churches count souls saved—or at least in attendance. The more we do, the bigger the numbers, the more value we have. The need for productivity has outstripped our ability to enjoy the gifts of the day.

Not all of life is quantifiable. Much that gives life meaning and adds richness to the human experience cannot be measured. How do we assess the productivity of the mother who sits at her sick child's bedside or the working couple who values their relationship enough to make love instead of mowing the lawn, cleaning the house, or closing another business deal? How would we measure the importance of time an artist or scientist uses to ponders new ideas? We would not call any of these activities productive because we are unable to quantify them. Yet they add a richness and depth to life that makes life worth living. When did these activities become countercultural?

DOING NOTHING

The intense drive to be productive makes the incubation stage seem particularly difficult, even for the artist. Incubation calls on the artist to do nothing, to cease productivity, and to wait—for God only knows how long—for a solution to the creative challenge. Turning conscious attention to the creative challenge at this stage only makes the solution disappear. Like dim constellations seen out of the corner of the eye on a starry night, the solution vanishes when viewed directly. Though tempted to do further research or wrestle with various solutions, the artist in the midst of the incubation stage holds the problem gently in the heart where it can rest undisturbed.

Holy Leisure

The church mothers and fathers knew the importance of doing nothing. They called it holy leisure. Things of a spiritual nature take time to develop and cannot grow if we are too busy. Productivity and busyness are not virtues in matters of the Spirit; loving God is.

Jesus said the first commandment is to love the Lord with all our heart, soul, mind, and strength. Love like this takes time to grow and cannot happen in the midst of frantic busyness or obsessive productivity, even busyness in the name of God. Without moments of holy leisure or sabbath, we risk losing our way as pilgrims on the inner journey, and the outer journey becomes absolutely meaningless. Sacred leisure frees us from our compulsiveness by rooting our work and our lives in the love of God. It reminds us that we are loved without needing to earn that love.

The incubation stage teaches us about holy leisure. Because it becomes necessary to cease working on the creative challenge in order for something new to be conceived, this stage invites us to take a break, kick off our shoes, and play.

My beautiful stepdaughter gave me a piece of calligraphy that invites me to include holy leisure in my schedule. It reads, "Some days are simply meant for playing." I keep this treasured gift where I can see it several times each day. It brings me back to the immeasurable truth when I start to stray from the pilgrim's path: divine love holds us even when we are not busily trying to hold onto it. God's creative Word has been at work in the world since before time came into being, and God is still at work today. Love's power, already unleashed in the world and in our lives, continuously transforms us all. Even when we are not actively building up God's reign or filling our days with ceaseless prayer, love works in our lives.

Our job as pilgrims is finding ways to cooperate with God's creative Word. Sometimes that means to cease striving and relax. The world will not stop turning if we take a break. There are things the Holy One cannot do until we get out of the way—like dismantling the false self.

The incubation stage of the creative process reassures us that doing nothing is okay; we are still valued even when we are not busy. This stage opens the possibility of enjoying life's gifts without having to produce them. It reveals to us that life, like creativity, is a gift offered freely to everyone.

Exercise

Out of Nothing

Measurement! It is the very foundation of the modern scientific method, the means by which the material world is admitted into existence.

—CANDACE B. PERT[1]

MATERIALS NEEDED
holy leisure
24 sequential hours

Back in the days when I was just beginning to recover from raging workaholism, my spiritual director suggested I go on a silent retreat once a month. Initially I used the time apart to write sermons or read, but soon the solitude and silence developed into holy leisure. I napped, read novels, took long walks by a flowing river, and I began sketching landscapes. Those retreats were just the right prescription for this weary soul. They restored sanity to a life out of control with work and helped me move closer to finding the place of my own resurrection.

Spend some time doing nothing productive. Daydream about being happy. Do something you enjoyed doing as a child. Take a day for holy leisure.

Crucible of Detachment

Father, if you are willing, remove this cup from me;
yet, not my will but yours be done.

—LUKE 22:42

In the incubation stage, continuing to seek a solution to the creative challenge actually becomes counterproductive for the artist. After the initial preparation and brainstorming, after trying various solutions "on for size" and arriving at several dead ends, when the frustration mounts and the fight-or-flight hormones course through the bloodstream, it is time to back off. Releasing the desired outcome, the artist must disengage from the original vision that initiated the work of art. Though the artist may be in love with the work's potential, letting go of the hoped-for outcome makes room for fresh creativity in the crucible of detachment.

LETTING GO—AGAIN AND AGAIN

Artists at this stage are like parents watching their child go away to college. The one they have guided, trained, pleaded with, cried over, rejoiced with, disciplined, and loved will leave their immediate supervision. Though letting a child go is difficult, they must or they will never know what this beloved child might become on her own. Their child will be exposed to many things beyond their control; she will begin to shape her life into what she alone chooses along with the unseen guidance of God. If the parents refuse to let her go, they will only stunt their child's growth. Out of love, they do the hard work of releasing the one they adore.

As the guardian of a work of art in process, the artist must deliberately detach from actively seeking a solution to the creative challenge. Like parents stepping back from the child's daily decisions, the artist allows the project to rest undisturbed. The lessons in letting go from the frustration stage may be practiced during incubation. For artists or pilgrims, releasing, detaching, surrendering, letting go—whatever name we call it—is never easy. We have to rehearse it again and again.

Taking a Break

I am enormously proud of a large painting in our family room. It is the best work I have done to date. When I look at it, I am still amazed that it came out of me; I sometimes check the signature just to be sure it did. While working on this canvas, whenever I felt I had pushed myself to the limits of my talent, ideas, and frustration, I stopped painting. I cleaned my brushes and did something entirely different, totally turning my thoughts, emotions, and activities in a new direction. Instead of my usual stewing over a problem in the painting, I did something I enjoyed. Removing myself from the source of frustration and stress, I took a break.

I established two criteria for the break: I had to enjoy the activity, and it had to take my mind off the frustration with the painting. This practice represented a radical change for me. Out of habit, I used to chain myself to the canvas until it was done. I developed this way of working in college when the painting I began at midnight was due the next morning at eight. In those days, I fussed and fumed until I finished. The new practice of stepping back and deliberately detaching from the project felt like a big sigh. All the pent-up frustration drained from my body as I began a different activity. I must have entered the incubation stage twenty times or more during this one painting.

This stage over which the artist has no control beyond its initiation is mysterious and mystical. The subconscious goes to work once the conscious mind gets out of the way. Like life growing unseen in the darkness of the womb, creativity generates in the distant corners of the artist's mind, coming into consciousness only when fully formed.

Discovering a Way to Proceed

Each time I returned to the canvas after taking a break, I brought a new idea that had come to me without my searching for it, while I was doing something else. The idea did not immediately surface as I began an alternative activity; sometimes it came the next morning as I brushed my hair or did the morning dishes. Without fail, the way to proceed beyond the place I perceived as the limit of my talent always came to me. I did not make it up or make it happen; it arrived through a nonlinear process. I could not have logically thought my way to the new creative idea, which I carried back to the painting. I know because I have tried. Before my work on this painting, I strained to think my way rationally out of situations where my talent and creativity were stuck but to no avail.

Pushing the River

When my friend Beth tries desperately to make something go her way that is not about to happen in this lifetime, she calls it "pushing the river." We know this phenomenon as "beating your head against the wall." When we try to manipulate circumstances and events to reach a desired outcome or hold so tightly to what we want that we cannot see anything else, we are pushing the river. This obsessive and compulsive behavior causes us to miss wonderful opportunities. It narrows our focus by placing blinders on our vision of what might be. Instead of going with the flow of life's current, we try to swim upstream by our own effort. If we could only let go and sail in the direction the energy of our days takes us, we would have the time of our life.

An artist in the flow of the creative process finds "happy accidents" enhance the work. "Happy accidents," those unplanned gifts of creativity, rather than looking like mistakes, turn out to resemble brilliant ideas. Before I began deliberately stepping back from the canvas at the point of an impasse, the accidents in my paintings never looked happy. I painted over them. The incubation stage for the artist rehearses detachment. With each work, the artist releases personal desires for the canvas, the song, the story and waits for what might be better than the artist's vision.

As pilgrims on the inner journey we learn to detach too. Usually we let go of our desires, learning to hold them lightly and with open hands, only after pushing the river a few hundred times. It often takes many attempts at pushing the river before it even occurs to us to think of releasing the desired outcome. Some pilgrims do this with more ease than others but only after having practiced. Initially on the inner journey, we want what we want, and we want God to give it to us now! No matter how great our desire for the Divine to show us a way, open a door, fix a relationship, change our life, or give us what we think we want, if we cannot detach and intentionally step back from the inner struggle, we may only make matters worse.

Once in high school, I badly wanted to go to a dance but had no prospects for a date. I had my eyes on a really cute boy I knew only from a distance; I wanted him to take me. My mother and I decided to do an experiment. Every night for a month we prayed. Like the persistent widow in Jesus' parable who daily badgered the judge for justice, we asked God to fulfill my desire. The day that cute boy appeared at my door with an invitation to the dance, I nearly jumped for glee. Eagerly I anticipated the dance and all the fun we would have. Was I wrong! I had an awkward and painful time. Not only did we have little in common, but we did not dance much. It could not have been much fun for him either.

The experience taught me two significant lessons: (1) be careful what you pray for, and (2) stop trying to push the river. Follow the timeless wisdom of recovery circles everywhere: "let go and let God." Who knows what might have happened had I not so stubbornly prayed for that one boy to ask me out? If I had stepped back and detached, I might have experienced something better, something God had in mind for my life instead of what I thought I wanted. It certainly would not have been any worse.

Surrendering Our Wants

The pilgrim's journey teaches us to trust God's love enough to let go of our wants and desires. We surrender our wishes long enough to see if they are what God has in mind for our lives. Whether struggling to make sense of the circumstances of our lives or desperately yearning for change, sometimes we can move forward only by detaching. Stepping back from the current behavior or circumstance to see what God will do is our only option when we have exhausted our efforts and the next step still remains unclear. If our spirits are clenched around a desire, we leave no room for God to give it to us, even if God yearns to do so.

Detachment is an important lesson on the spiritual journey, challenging the pilgrim from a very early age. My two-year-old grandson demonstrated the difficulty of letting go when we were dining in a restaurant. After he finished the tomatoes on his salad plate, the server removed the plate to make room for his spaghetti. My redheaded grandson adores both these foods. He began to cry as soon as he realized his salad plate was gone. We tried to explain he was about to get spaghetti, but it did not matter. He wailed, "But I liked it!" as he threw his little face into his hands. For him, the absence of his salad plate was the end of all his enjoyment; he wanted it back! Within minutes, much to the relief of those dining in the restaurant, the bowl of spaghetti appeared before him, miraculously mending his very real broken heart.

Letting go of that which we desire distresses us greatly, especially when we do not know whether anything better waits around the corner—or when it might arrive. It takes a lifetime to learn to detach from our deepest desires, but as serious pilgrims, we must. The cross is after all a sign of letting go, of ultimate surrender. For the pilgrim on the inner journey who follows the way of the cross, letting go makes room for God in our lives. If we are lucky, when we let go of our last earthly breath, we will have practiced letting go thousands of times.

Exercise

Turning It Over

I can't make the river come to me,
I can't keep it from flowing away.
Just drink the water like it's holy,
it brings a bit of growing my way.

—STEVE GARNAAS-HOLMES[2]

MATERIALS NEEDED
crayons or colored makers
18" x 24" drawing paper

Detaching from our desires is one of the more difficult things we do in life. A friend of mine shared with me the following prayer, which helps me unclench my fists from around my longings: "God, please give me what I want or something better." I have prayed it so many times, it has left a permanent wrinkle in my brain.

Think about a time in your life when you have wanted something to happen in the worst way and it did not materialize. How did you feel? What did you do to try to make it happen? Did you give up yearning for it or do you still crave it?

Get out your crayons or markers and draw what you desire in your life now. What is your deep longing at the moment? What do you wish would happen in your life? Try to draw this desire without using words. Remember, it is not important that this creative attempt look like a masterpiece. Create from your soul.

When you have finished, find a way to offer the drawing and the situation to God. Turn the drawing face side down as a gesture of "turning it over" to God. Or place the drawing on a home altar to signify letting go of the desire. When all else fails, try praying, "God, please manifest this desire in my life or give me something better."

Wait a Minute

*Now faith is the assurance of things hoped for, the
conviction of things not seen.*

—HEBREWS 11:1

My father, now in his eighties, has taught me about waiting.
Each summer we go fishing in the Chincoteague Bay. He loves
to fish, and I love being on the water with him. The morning
of the fishing trip, we load all our supplies, including enough
bait to last a week. Sometimes when we are on the boat, the
fish almost jump aboard. As soon as we lower a line in the
water, we pull it back out again with a fish flopping on the
hook. Those days are really fun. More frequently, however,
long pauses intervene between the nibbles, and each of us
gets lost in the abundant silence. Though our thoughts may
take us a thousand miles away, my dad remains alert to the
slightest tug on the line. He never forgets he is waiting for a
fish. Consequently he always catches the first or largest fish of
the day. I do not know how he does this with such consistency;
I suspect it has to do with the quality of his waiting.

Over the years I have noticed a difference in our fishing
styles. When nothing is biting, I tend to think some sea creature has stolen my bait. I check the line more frequently than
my father checks his. Dad waits patiently for the fish to get
hungry, trusting his bait remains on the hook. Minimally, he
expects to catch his supper even as he holds out hope for a
much larger haul, as evidenced by the amount of bait we take

along on each expedition. Maybe his years of living make him more patient at fishing or maybe his temperament makes the difference. I am hoping for the former reason because then there is hope for me. Whatever the reason, I want to learn to wait like he does. He waits with expectation and hope, open to the slightest nibble on the line and ready to act when it comes along.

AN ART TO BE LEARNED

The incubation stage of the creative process is like waiting for a fish to bite. When this stage goes well, the artist resembles my father fishing. While thinking about other matters, the artist remains attentive to the slightest inbreaking of creative thought. Wanting to reel in a fresh idea, the artist waits, expecting to catch an idea that will clear the way through the frustration and on to a finished work of art. Over time, the artist learns the only way through the frustration is to let go of the struggle and wait, trusting good things will come to those who don't pull their line out of the water too frequently. Sometimes tempted to believe a solution to the creative challenge can be hurried, artists obsess over all the possible answers and try to think through to resolution. This results in a dead end and only slows down the process, though it may take a while to figure that out.

Waiting is an art to be learned. In the midst of the incubation stage, the artist doesn't know whether an idea will emerge as the catch of a lifetime or not. The myriad of possible solutions may never yield one that works. There is no promise the detachment of the incubation stage will produce art. Experience teaches the artist to recognize waiting as the most likely way to arrive at the sterling solution for the creative challenge. But without guarantees, waiting becomes very difficult.

The artist who trusts the workings of creativity in the incubation stage waits with an actively receptive and hopeful attitude rather than in a passive or resigned frame of mind. Waiting, ready to receive an idea that will lead to the next stage of the creative process, the artist hopes the answer will come sooner rather than later.

When the artist's livelihood depends on producing art or when a deadline looms, waiting with the clock ticking in the background wears on the nerves like fingernails scraping on a chalkboard. The pressure of time diminishes the quality of waiting, and waiting in the incubation stage—like good prayer and great fishing—is best done in unhurried time.

INCUBATION OF THE SOUL

Pilgrims frequently face extended intervals of waiting. The Israelites waited for forty years to be led into the land flowing with milk and honey. As contemporary pilgrims we often wait for the way to be made clear. We wait to be shown what to do next with our lives and how to love better. We wait for troublesome times to be met with days of ease. Waiting for deliverance while in the midst of tribulation is never easy. Ancient cultures often viewed times of trial as an incubation period when the pilgrim experienced a great inner transformation. Even if we believe an inner transformation occurs during our painful times, waiting can still feel like forty years in the wilderness. As pilgrims in search of the place of our own resurrection, like artists in the incubation stage of the creative process, we wait with no guarantee a way will open soon.

The pilgrim's incubation stage, often synonymous with the dark night of the soul, transforms the pilgrim's identity under the cover of darkness. In the obscurity of the dark void, the Divine Lover frees the true self and brings the soul to a place of radical receptivity.

We are not in control of the incubating self; rather, God does this work. The pilgrim may be tempted to rush through the dark night because the experience feels awful and arduous. But avoidance only prolongs the misery. The time in the dark night lasts as long as it takes to heal the pilgrim's soul. If we want to experience the resurrection, we must first go through the crucifying darkness where the false self is dismantled. The caterpillar cannot fly without going through the transforming darkness of the cocoon, and then as a butterfly, struggling free of it. Pilgrims must trudge through the despair and do the accompanying grief work. Skipping the gut-wrenching feelings is not an option. We can either go kicking and screaming, resisting the tribulation with every muscle in our being, or we can learn to wait, trusting God is present in our time of trial. The quality of waiting on the spiritual journey significantly affects our experience of this inner transformation.

In the Company of Others

Holding on by my fingernails, I waited for my dark night to be over. Had it not been for the faith and prayers of my family and community, I am not sure I would have survived. Their witness and belief in the God of resurrection carried me for many months. On the numerous days when I could not trust my own faith, I could trust the faith of those who prayed for me. When it seemed as if nothing was happening and I was stuck in despair, a word of encouragement came from a member of my community reminding me that I was held in the palm of God's hand. Though I could not wait with faith or hope, they could; so I relied upon them. Waiting for God to make a way through the darkness is nearly impossible to do alone. We need a community of believers who will wait with us as we experience this raw transformation; for only those who have survived a journey into the void can attest with any authority that these times do come to an end.

Looking back, I understand I could not have rushed through this darkness. In fact, my spiritual director told me not to hurry through this trial. Just like the gestation of a baby, incubation of the soul takes time. A community of believers who will wait with us for our true self to unfold provides a light in the midst of our darkness. Like midwives, they recognize signs of life stirring when we cannot see clearly because of the pain. They hold the vision of what we are becoming when we are blind to it. They call forth our best self, our truest self, by their very presence and coach us into wholeness. Waiting is less lonely when passed in the midst of a community; and even though others cannot lift the pain from our life, their presence makes the waiting a little more bearable. It also helps if they know how to fish.

Exercise

Something to Do While Waiting

Body and soul, we wait for new life to make us everlastingly alive, new blood to flow through our dusty and sorrowing world, soft as rainwater and almost without taste but with the faintest tinge of sweetness to it.

—FREDERICK BUECHNER[3]

MATERIALS NEEDED
   18" x 24" drawing paper
   crayons or colorful makers

I hold in my mind the image of a little bird on a nest—an image symbolic of my emerging true self. I imagine the bird patiently waiting through all kinds of weather for her eggs to hatch. In my mind, I am both the bird and the egg.

What images come to you that represent the emergence of your true self? Draw one now using your nondominant hand. Listen to your intuition. Choose the colors that attract you. Place them on the page where they seem to belong. Take as long as you need. Let the Spirit guide you.

Entertaining Strangers

Do not neglect to show hospitality to strangers, for by doing that some have entertained angels without knowing it.

—Hebrews 13:2

When I was a child, the neighborhood kids wanted to hang out at my house even though we did not have all the latest toys. During my teen years, my friends secretly confessed to me how they wished their parents were more like mine. With open arms and welcoming hearts, my parents have always made space for others in their home, treating everyone with love and respect regardless of age, social standing, race, or religion. Both of my folks innately know how to put a person at ease, which makes guests feel welcomed and appreciated. Sharing the finest of what they have as well as the best of who they are, my parents have the spiritual gift of hospitality.

Hospitality, a Generous Act of Love

Living under their roof, I not only witnessed my parents' gift of hospitality shared with others, I received it. "The classic elements of hospitality offered to guests are food and drink, shelter and rest, protection and care, enjoyment and peace," writes Marjorie Thompson in *Soul Feast*.[4] In addition to offering these elements, my folks provided two other ingredients of hospitality—love and generosity. These fundamental elements of their spiritual gift allowed my brothers and me to be and become the persons God intended.

When my brothers and I were in college, we often came home for weekend visits. At the end of the weekend Mom and Dad loaded up the car with groceries, packed up snacks for the four-hour trip back to school, gave us gas money, and asked if we needed anything else. We always went back to school with more than we had taken home. My brothers used to joke that if we delayed our good-byes long enough, the kitchen sink would be in the backseat of the car before we pulled out of the driveway.

The spiritual gift of hospitality is a generous act of love. It makes friends out of offspring and family out of strangers by creating a space for them to feel safe, welcomed, and nurtured. The space may be a physical room, but more likely it will be an emotional atmosphere of love, freedom, and safety, the kind of atmosphere my parents provided for my brothers and me.

HOSPITALITY OF TIME

The principles of hospitality are keenly applicable for artists in the midst of the creative process. The ideas that come to artists often seem like complete strangers rather than anything originating within ourselves. New ideas seemingly emerge from out of nowhere, surprising and delighting us the way new friendships enchant us. As the artist nurtures the idea into form, it becomes a cherished companion—so much so that completing a work of art compares to parting with a trusted friend.

Learning how to be hospitable to the ideas that desire expression in the world comprises a critical part of creativity. In the incubation stage, the artist works to create the kind of atmosphere that will give birth to the best solution to the creative challenge. Some of us clean our studios and go to movies; others go on walks or take long drives through the country. Every artist creates hospitable space in a unique way, but one element of hospitality holds true for everyone. Creativity takes time. It cannot be forced or coerced; it has to emerge. Creating hospitable space for creative ideas to unfold requires a great deal of unstructured time.

In my early years of ministry, I complained to my wonderful pastoral counselor about the amount of downtime or unscheduled time I needed but was not getting. From my perspective, my need seemed greater than that of my colleagues. I confessed feeling guilty over this because free time appeared extravagant and self-indulgent in the face of the multiple needs facing my parishioners. My counselor gave me sage advice. He said simply and directly, "Take the time you need; you can live with the guilt." He explained that creative people often need abundant unscheduled time because so much happens under the surface of their lives. All kinds of ideas germinate in the deeper layers of one's being, activity not obvious to the casual observer. Thanks to him, I learned to be hospitable to the creativity sprouting in my subconscious and my soul. And the guilt lessened over time. Had I followed the example set by my busier colleagues, I might have trampled on many creative ideas before they had a chance to make themselves known.

The Creative Life Yearning to Live in You

Not only artists need to be hospitable toward their creative ideas. Pilgrims need to practice this essential virtue too. Hospitality gives birth to the creative life desiring to live in each of us. Our true self, the creative part of us, needs much love, nurture, safety, and freedom in order to grow. In a society that undervalues creativity and other right-brain functions, the creativity within us often remains a stranger, a part of us that feels unknown and unaffirmed.

In the ancient Near East, strict hospitality codes bound individuals to provide the necessities of life to traveling strangers. What if today we lived by hospitality codes obligating us to honor the life trying to be born in us? What would it look like if, compelled by love for our buried creativity, we provided unhurried time for its development? How would our life be different if we were generous and hospitable to our truest self, granting it nourishment and space to emerge? What if we appreciated our own creativity the way the great Creator God appreciates creativity? Who might we be and what might we do if we were hospitable to the authentic self within us?

Learning to be hospitable to the creativity inside is the only sensible thing to do once we realize our creativity mirrors God's creativity. Anything less betrays faithfulness to God's desire for our life. My stepdaughter, in her twenties, is pursuing a career in performance. She confided in me that in order to give an audience a great performance, she needs some external stimulation to fill her creative spirit. She reads voraciously, goes to movies, and attends live performances whenever possible. At such a young age she already has figured out how to welcome her inner creativity. What if we all listened deeply to the creative stranger within us? What if we treated this neglected part of ourselves as an honored guest? How would our lives be different if the authentic, creative self within became a trusted friend?

WELCOMING GOD

The spiritual pilgrim who develops the gift of hospitality toward inner creativity welcomes the presence of the Living God. As we invite the use of our creativity, we receive our Maker's creativity within us. Though we seldom think about providing hospitality for God, that is why we are created. Our bodies are temples that house Divine Love. On the spiritual journey the pilgrim embodies greater amounts of God's love until it shines through unimpeded by the false self.

For God's love to shine through, we pilgrims must be emptied of our attachments—whatever prevents us from receiving the love of God. Attachments are those habitual behaviors and beliefs that cause us to do what we do not want to do and to avoid what we wish we would do. We may be attached to the belief that we have to earn our place in life, behave to meet others' expectations, or martyr ourselves in order to achieve holiness. Whatever our attachment, it is tied to the assumption that we can achieve happiness by our own efforts. Since God is our only true source of happiness, none of our attachments will ever permanently satisfy us. As the Divine Lover frees us from our attachments, we become increasingly hospitable to the presence of God within us and within the world.

SEMINAL SOUL WORK

Only the Divine can rid us of our attachments, those unconscious motivations for happiness to which we cling. We cannot do this by our efforts alone. If we could, we would probably mess things up. In what is essentially a hands-off time for the pilgrim, God uses life's difficulties to keep us busy while the really important soul work continues. Distracted by daily affairs, we are less likely to ruin the new thing God is doing in bringing forth our truest self.

In the season of incubation the Holy One works to bring to birth our immensely precious and valuable true self. During the dark night, we pilgrims become more hospitable to divine love and to the life that wants to be lived in us. As we are transformed, our true self—no longer a stranger to us—becomes a trusted friend. This seminal soul work prepares us to live a new life, one more in keeping with our heart's deepest desires.

Exercise

Generous Friends

Bear witness to the love of God in this world,
so that those to whom love is a stranger
will find in you generous friends.

—SERVICE OF CHRISTIAN MARRIAGE
THE UNITED METHODIST BOOK OF WORSHIP[5]

MATERIALS NEEDED
journal and pen

When traveling, my husband and I love staying at bed-and-breakfasts. Our favorite B and Bs are the ones where the owners know how to be hospitable. They know just when to interact with their guests and when to leave them alone.

If you were both the owner and the guest at a B and B, in what ways would you offer hospitality to yourself? How would you receive it? What do you need to encourage your becoming the person God intends you to be?

Write in your journal what you need on your pilgrim's path and make a commitment to honor that need.

Do something hospitable for yourself today. Light a candle. Say a prayer. Take a bubble bath. Go fishing. Visit an art gallery or paint.

Illumination

Love the Mystery

*Very truly, I tell you, when you were younger, you
used to fasten your own belt and to go wherever you
wished. But when you grow old, you will stretch out
your hands, and someone else will fasten a belt
around you and take you where you do not wish to go.*

—John 21:18

One of my nephews enjoys taking things apart, always curious about what's inside. As a child, he could be busy for hours disassembling discarded electronics. Always surprised by the shapes and colors found inside the casing, he treasured the pieces of metal and strands of wire. My brother and sister-in-law had to keep a close eye on their son because his unrestrained curiosity could easily have caused them to lose the family television.

Taken by Surprise

The natural curiosity of children awes me. Their willingness to be surprised by new ideas and new knowledge allows them to approach life without the arrogance of an adult with all the answers. They live each day with an openness to the mysterious. As I watch my grandchildren, I notice their captivation with the world around them. A ladybug holds their awareness for an eternity as it creeps across their small, stubby fingers. They do not care that the little red bug with black spots is a friendly insect, eating the aphids that devour our garden; they are enraptured by its beauty and the delicate sensation of its trek across their fingertips. My grandchildren want to know where it lives and where it flies and why. They ask an infinite number of "whys."

Children are undisturbed when their last "why" trumps their guardian's knowledge because they delight in the mystery. The largeness of life that lies beyond anyone's explanation is a child's playground. For my grandchildren—and for all children enthralled with God's creation—the joy is found in the mystery.

Somewhere in our growing up we lose our enchantment with the unexplainable. Mystery becomes a puzzle to be solved. Like learning to read or to ride a bike, mystery presents another area of life over which to gain mastery. Years of solving mysteries and accumulating knowledge slowly send our curiosity into the background, making it difficult for us to be easily surprised. Our need for certitude replaces our love for surprise, until we can no longer love the mystery or abandon ourselves to it the way we did as children.

In our quest for certainty, we learn to categorize and then to prejudge people, situations, and even God on the basis of those categories. This is not necessarily a bad skill. Without a certain amount of categorizing, we probably would be unable to handle the vast amount of information we encounter in a lifetime. Unfortunately, the act of categorizing decreases our openness to truth, especially if the truth we seek lies outside the realm of our experience. Openness to truth diminishes in proportion to our dwindling willingness to be taken by surprise.

My nephew, an adolescent now, still takes things apart for sheer enjoyment. One of the lucky ones, he carried his curiosity with him into the teenage years. Artists are lucky too. Somehow they negotiate their way from childhood to adulthood with curiosity intact. For the artist, a willingness to be surprised is so much more important than the need for certitude. Maybe that is what Einstein meant when he said, "Imagination is more important than knowledge." Imagination keeps us open to possibilities and to surprise the way curiosity does, and the openness to surprise makes the "Aha!" moment possible.

AHA!

The "Aha!" moment—the surprise in the creative process—occurs during the illumination stage. Most everyone has experienced an "Aha!" moment, finding a solution to a problem from out of the blue at a time when our attention was focused elsewhere. The insight of the "Aha!" moment comes out of nowhere through a nonlinear process. It appears by a seemingly mysterious force. For the artist, such a moment clears a way for continuing the creative process; the energy to proceed accompanies the solution.

The "Aha!" moment gives artists a fresh perspective, coupled with the feeling that the new insight provides absolutely the best answer to the creative question. Though artists anticipate such an experience, the "Aha!" moment arrives with an air of surprise. It comes in its own time, fitting the creative puzzle at hand.

The "Aha!" moment (sometimes called the "Eureka!" moment), shows up at the doorstep of the creative process only after artists have struggled to find the appropriate answer and then relinquished the struggle. It comes without manipulation or effort. In order to experience an "Aha!" moment, artists must let the process take them where they did not intend to go by giving up control—not always an easy thing to accomplish.

CERTITUDE, A STUMBLING BLOCK TO FAITH

Wanting to control the outcome of a situation stems from our need for certitude. The more certainty we need as pilgrims, the more we will want to control. The more we want to control, the less open we are to surprise. Control and curiosity stand at opposite ends of the spectrum. Control limits possibilities and binds us like the Lilliputians bound Gulliver, one rope at a time, until we cannot move beyond the border of our own constraints. Curiosity, on the other hand, keeps us receptive to new experiences and to surprise. It calls us to venture over the horizon and helps us regain our childlike love of mystery.

On the pilgrim's inner journey, the dark night of the soul eventually gives way to a period of illumination. Our false self—along with some of its attachments—has been put to rest in the dark night. In the dawn of the illumination stage our truer self emerges, bringing the return of lightheartedness and ease. With the emergence of the true self comes a new awareness: we are not as much in control of our lives as we once thought. This awakening can make us question many certainties we have taken for granted even as it lessens our need for certitude.

Though we may not recognize the need to be sure as a stumbling block on the pilgrim's journey, this need produces a tremendous obstacle for the life of faith. Faith calls us to greater trust as we move along the spiritual path; the need to be certain inhibits trust and stymies our growth. The birth of the true self shrinks our need for certitude and opens the door to greater depths of love and faith.

One of my dear friends, when coming out of her darkest night, began calling God "The Great Whatever." She was no longer sure about the accuracy of her previous understanding of God, but she had not yet grown into a new way of knowing the Divine Lover. Her old understanding of God, of which she had been certain, had grown too small. It had limited her ability to love and be loved. In the dark night, the Divine Lover invited my friend to deeper levels of trust, radically transforming her relationship with God. With the onset of the illumination stage, a different way of knowing the Divine Lover slowly surfaced yet remained somewhat undefined. "The Great Whatever" seemed to be the most honest way of addressing her Creator. Trading in her certitude for the possibility of greater freedom, more love, and a return to the awareness of mystery, my friend faces a life full of surprises.

GLIMPSES OF GIFTS

Illumination does not always come quickly to the pilgrim. When it does arrive, an element of obscurity lingers. The dawn after the dark night brings only glimpses of God's transforming work in our lives. We almost never get the full picture. The light of day reveals a place on our journey where we did not plan to go. Though not conscious of our choice to ever go here, our soul somehow, somewhere said yes to God's transforming work. This new, freer place holds an awareness of our own limitations. We know we could never have arrived here by our efforts alone. Through the generous grace of the Divine Lover, our pilgrim journey has brought us to a place more spacious and more loving than what we knew before the onset of our experience of the dark night.

In the illumination period of the spiritual journey, pilgrims receive a blessed awareness of the gifts given in the dark night. These gifts previously hidden from us enrich the quality of our days. Our creative energies increase. We are freer to love with our whole heart instead of parceling out love based on what we can afford to lose. This liberation to love others comes out of the awareness that we are deeply and passionately loved by God. In the light of the new day, we possess an inkling that the love flowing through us comes straight from the Inexhaustible Source.

Our new creativity replaces our need to know how life will turn out with a willingness to be surprised by the adventure of living. By the grace of God we are released from our old compulsion to be certain into the arms of Love, the most excellent Mystery ever. Once again, we find we are like children, open to the joy found in mystery.

Exercise

Confusion or Joy? You Choose!

> *Confusion happens when mystery is an enemy and
> we feel we must solve it to master our destinies.*
>
> —GERALD G. MAY[1]

MATERIALS NEEDED
color copy of a favorite photo
scissors
glue stick
8½" x 11" white paper
colorful markers
journal and pen

My husband and I recently moved to a rural setting after years
of city living. Every day feels like an adventure out of the pages
of *National Geographic*. We see lizards with tails of lapis blue,
yellow and pink-striped moths, and black snakes mating on
our driveway. We watch deer eat from the persimmon tree in
our front yard and witness the playful curiosity of a small
grey fox. Hawks, owls, wild turkey, and bluebirds glide silently
through our backyard. My husband and I are transported into
delight by symphonies of birds and frogs, and we dance under
skies brilliant with pulsating lightning bugs. Like children in
a game of peekaboo, we revel in the mysterious appearance of
each new creature as our hearts fill with gratitude for the Love
that created them.

Make an enlarged color copy of a favorite photograph
and cut it into many small squares. With a glue stick arrange
the pieces on white paper to create an abstract design. Instead

of trying to reproduce the original picture, think in terms of colors, textures, and pattern. Make a mosaic out of all the pieces, a new image out of the old.

When it is finished, compare your mosaic to the original photograph. Though the images in the photo mosaic may be confused, can you appreciate the beauty of your new creation? If your eye searches for clues to turn this mosaic into the old photo, reproduce your mosaic on another sheet of paper using colorful markers. Now what do you experience?

In your journal, record what you have learned through this exercise. What feelings surfaced as you cut up the original image? What did you experience as you arranged the pieces of the photo into a mosaic? What was it like to draw the mosaic with colorful markers?

Conversations with God

*We have this treasure in clay jars, so that it may be
made clear that this extraordinary power belongs to
God and does not come from us. We are afflicted in
every way, but not crushed; perplexed, but not driven
to despair; persecuted, but not forsaken; struck down,
but not destroyed.*

—2 CORINTHIANS 4:7-9

I have a conversation with God when I write or paint.
Sometimes I loudly voice strong opinions as the Divine Listener
allows me to get things off my chest. Other times, God does the
talking and my job is to listen. When God talks, the part of me
that pontificates—my ego-self—eavesdrops on a conversation
between the Divine Creator and my soul. In the face of such wisdom, my ego-self is rendered speechless; it can add nothing
substantial to the illuminating discourse it hears.

EAVESDROPPING ON THE TRUTH

As a pilgrim searching for the place of my own resurrection,
I believe God continuously converses with my soul-self, the
part of me that God has always intended for me to be. This
truest part remains hidden away, safe in Love's arms, until I am
ready to let it shine through me completely. My soul's conversation with the Holy One continues in ceaseless communion
like a sonnet spoken by two lovers—though most of the time

I know nothing about it. Only through the gift of creative expression, in eavesdropping moments of grace, do I sense a conversation occurring at all. With a flash of insight I am privy to truth so universal and simultaneously so intimately personal that it meets my exact need while meeting the needs of the world. The insight I receive in a moment of illumination, imbued with vitality and healing, contains God's truth. In such moments, moisture soaks into the parched places of my life. What was dying regains energy. Whenever I am privileged to overhear a conversation between God and my soul, the art I make conveys more universal meaning than the creative works of my dumbstruck ego. This deeply meaningful art comes wrapped up in the Creator's creativity and blessed into being in ways I could not manage on my own.

Unfortunately, not all my creative endeavors contain divine wisdom; much that I have written and painted has been solely the product of my own ego and its shadow side. Some of it may be considered good art but not great art. The truth contained within these creations distinctively differs from the wisdom that emerges out my soul's conversation with the Divine Creator; the truth is smaller and less universal. Making ego-centered art feels labor-intensive with no sense of ease or flow about the work. The illuminating moment is absent, and art making becomes like jackhammering through concrete with a nail file. I think I am allowed to have times like these in order to remember from whom the deeper creativity comes.

Getting the Ego out of the Way

If I am astute enough to recognize an absence of the "Aha!" experience while I am still creating, sometimes I move beyond this laborious process simply by relaxing, letting go, and per-severing. Writing in a stream of consciousness for several pages or doing several preliminary drawings will often open the way to my soul's voice, and, if I am fortunate, God's voice. Using my nondominant hand to write or paint accomplishes the same thing. Something about simple repetition and using my less-coordinated hand moves my ego out of the way. Perhaps my ego gets bored easily by routine and does not want to take credit for the mess made by my clumsier hand. When my ego quits pontificating, the still small voice within has a better chance of being heard. I wait and hope for this opportunity. One "Aha!" moment can keep me inspired for weeks. It keeps the creative process alive and infused with meaning. Accompanied by a deep sense of peace, these illumi-native, meaning-filled moments—though brief—seem time-less. For a short period of time, with the ego receding into the background, I am not conscious of myself at all. Only the cre-ativity coming through me exists, and that is all that matters.

GLIMPSES OF GRACE

On a small scale, the artist experiences in the "Aha!" moment what the pilgrim knows on a larger scale. Reality is more than what can be perceived through the senses, and grace—like creativity—abounds. In the pilgrim's illuminative moment, God breaks through ordinary life to reveal a deeper, everlast-ing reality. The pilgrim becomes one with the God of Love as time appears to stand still.

This kind of experience opens us to a larger reality than we have known previously. For a little while, in the eternal now, all the barriers of time, space, and ego that separate us from God and one another dissolve. We lose any sense of where self leaves off and Creator begins. United with God and all of God's creation, we are lost to self and found in God. We get a glimpse of grace woven through every leaf, floating in each oxygen molecule, and emanating from the heart of even the most unlovely. This kind of grace holds us when life beats us down. And we find we are not destroyed.

I remember a time of horrible confusion when I did not know whom or what I could trust. In a moment of despair, I confided in my mother that I no longer knew what the truth was. She replied without skipping a breath, "The only truth there is, is God's love." An illuminative experience opens us to God's truth. We know in those few minutes of transcending grace more than we knew only moments before. More than just head knowledge, it is knowing with the heart and with every cell of the body. We never forget this kind of knowledge because the memory attaches into our DNA. With the power of a religious conversion, an illuminative experience changes the way we perceive life. Nothing will ever be the same; nor do we want it to be.

Shortly after I confessed my inner state of confusion to my mother, I had an illumination. I call it my divine surprise. Like John Wesley, who had his heart "strangely warmed" in a service of worship at Aldersgate Street in 1738, I experienced my heart being strangely warmed too. I awoke one night from a dream and after going to the bathroom, I got back in bed. Fully awake, I noticed my chest over my heart area was warm. Curious, I wondered if this sensation was my flesh or just a warm emotion left over from my dream. I touched my skin. It was physically warmer than the surrounding area, and it continued to grow warmer. The heat I felt was accompanied by an expanding state of bliss, the way you feel when you have fallen deeply in love. As blissful feelings increased, I gave myself over to them. There was nothing else I wanted to do or could do. I merged with the Bliss, feeling totally loved and totally in love with God. Not knowing where I left off and God began, I felt one with the Divine Lover. The next morning, sated with Love, I awoke with a new sense of inner peace. All my striving and anxieties had evaporated in the night. In the ripening afterglow, God embraced the new tenderness within me. In ways I had not previously known or imagined, Love encircled me. Peace prevailed in the days that followed and still remains today.

It Is All about Love

Describing such a divine surprise or what comes from it is nearly impossible. There are no words adequate to the task. I feel dumbstruck, and my attempts are feeble at best. If I were a poet, I might better articulate the richness of the experience.

That illumination transformed me. Nothing is the same for me now; nor do I want anything to be the same. Just as John Wesley's heartwarming experience freed him from the prison of works righteousness, opening him to an experience of God's saving grace, so did my warmed heart open the way to a deeper loving relationship with God. If you ask me to articulate the truth of that transcendent moment, I will say, "Love. Love is all that matters. Love is all there is. God's truth is Love."

Exercise

Divine Surprises

However much we may know God, the great lesson to learn is that at any minute [God] may break in. We are apt to overlook this element of surprise, yet God never works in any other way.

—OSWALD CHAMBERS[2]

MATERIALS NEEDED
colorful markers
journal

I love pleasant surprises. I love giving them and receiving them. As a child I made May baskets and left them anonymously on the porch steps of my friends' houses. I love surprise birthday parties too. It is fun to see the expression on the face of the person turning a year older when everyone shouts, "Surprise!"

I think God must love surprises too, because our Creator breaks into my hectically scheduled day with a spectacular sunset or an unexpected gesture of kindness from a stranger. When we least expect it, the Divine Lover quietly shows us the power of love.

Using colorful markers, write several pages of your inner thoughts in your journal. It does not matter what you write. Simply write what you hear yourself thinking. No one will see this exercise. As you write, feel free to switch colors frequently if you like. The colors can help express your interior life. You do not have to write on lined paper or even make the letters all the same size. You can print part of the thoughts and use script for other sections. If images come to mind, draw them in your journal. Let the form and content come from within. The trick is to listen to the inner voice.

Sometimes divine surprises happen in the writing; sometimes they happen following the writing. Sometimes there are no surprises, just a cleaning of our inner thoughts. When you finish, look back over the pages. Are there any divine surprises?

Eyes to See and Ears to Hear

Blessed are your eyes, for they see, and your ears, for they hear.

—MATTHEW 13:16

It may take a long time for the artist to experience the illumination stage of the creative process, or it may just feel like a long time. The important though demanding work of the previous stages must not be minimized. Artists need courage and faith to wait for the onset of the "Aha!" moment. Though they might wish to schedule an insight the way one sets a luncheon date, the illuminating idea comes as a gift from God-only-knows-where, arriving in its own sweet time. Artists cannot hurry, manipulate, manage, or make it happen. When the "Aha!" moment descends upon the artist like long-awaited manna from heaven, creative blocks evaporate. An illumination sustains the artist immersed in the creative process in the way good food nourishes the body. Having feasted on insight, the creative juices to begin to flow once again.

THE SUBTLE "AHA!"

Young artists of any age, just beginning to follow the call of creativity, may need help recognizing the "Aha!" moment, especially if they expect the illuminating insight to be dramatic. Most often it is not sensational but very subtle. I discovered early in the exploration of my creativity that illuminations are not always abundantly clear. Once in a great while I knew with certainty that the insight received would work, but usually only with hindsight did I recognize the subtle hunch that provided the best course of action.

My tentativeness in recognizing an "Aha!" moment may have been related to my personality. I tend to wonder whether something better waits around the next corner. Will the proverbial grass be greener at a later date? I have come to accept this persistent second-guessing in myself. Over the years experience has taught me to go with my first hunch; it is usually filled with the most wisdom.

For the artist awakening to creativity's call, simple repetition develops a trained awareness of an illumination. Like a child learning the multiplication tables, repeatedly going through the process fixes it in the memory. Unfortunately, discerning a creative breakthrough is not always as clear-cut as learning two times two. Identifying the best solution to a creative challenge can involve some trial and error. A neon sign seldom marks the way for the artist stuck midway through the creative process. Discerning an illumination has as much to do with faith and trust as the rest of the creative process.

Learning to trust one's instincts and intuition is part of what it means to be an artist. To recognize the inner voice accurately takes a different kind of listening and a different kind of looking than most individuals usually employ. The subtlety of a creative breakthrough sometimes comes in a whisper, requiring us to pay close attention to nuances and listen under the surface of things. Perfecting the recognition of an illuminating insight can take the artist years.

LEARNING TO SEE

In my early explorations of creativity, talking to other artists and listening to my intuition aided my ability to identify which insight to pursue. Looking for the relationship between things and ideas instead of seeing them in a vacuum also proved to be valuable. Like putting on a pair of glasses with a new prescription, each time I looked for the "Aha!" moment, I saw it more clearly. When I thought an artistic hunch might pan out, I stepped out on faith. Following my intuition, I paid attention to how I felt and how far I got in the creative process. And I remembered the feeling when a hunch panned out.

The learning curve was not smooth; I followed plenty of hunches straight to dead ends. Instead of allowing a dead end to stop me in my tracks permanently, I returned to the incubation stage and waited. The waiting taught me about faith, much the way life teaches us about prayer. If the choices are to sink or swim, I choose to swim. Rather than fretting, I learned to have faith that the "Aha!" moment eventually would arrive. For the artist within me, it was the only and best choice I could make.

The path of the artist teaches us faith. In faith we wait to receive the creative breakthrough, and with faith we embark in the direction that breakthrough indicates. When all is said and done, faith is simply a way of seeing life.

Repetition proves to be a good teacher for pilgrims too. Remembering how God acted in our lives in the past helps us recognize the Divine Lover at work in the present. Sometimes it takes a few hundred times of seeing God work in familiar ways before we recognize Love at work. When I first began the practice of centering prayer, I did not know for certain whether God was in my prayer time. In fact, I practiced it for years before I began to identify the presence of God in the silence. Most of those early prayers felt very empty, and I acted in faith that I was communicating with the Holy One at all. Had it not been for the wisdom of the Christian community's collective memory, I might have given up the form of prayer that now feeds me daily. I knew that Christians had used silence as prayer for centuries; and I figured if it worked for them, it could work for me too. Trusting in the tradition of the church helped shape my way of seeing and hearing God in my prayer life.

The Collective Memory

On the pilgrim's journey, the gift of memory plays a significant role in discerning the Divine Lover at work in our lives and in the life of the world. In my meanderings, I have learned not to rely on my failing memory alone but to lean into the collective memory of the Christian community for support. It contains wisdom far greater than mine. The scriptures and church history record stories of God's saving love and share examples of how God has spoken to the faithful throughout the centuries. These sources magnify the scope of my solitary memory. By relying on the pool of wisdom found in the Christian tradition, all pilgrims draw from a deep well when discerning God's presence.

At the beginning of my faith journey, the collective memory of the church assisted me the most in discerning God's illuminating presence. I read of Saul's blinding experience and the angel's annunciation to Mary, but I also read about many persons of faith who had no blinding visions or angelic visitations accompanied by golden light. The majority of illuminations of grace on the pilgrim's path, though significant, are extremely subtle. In our incarnational faith, the Divine more often hides in flesh and blood than visibly showing off through a display of exuberant mysticism. A healing word from a friend, the guidance of a spiritual director, or a life well lived by a faithful believer are means by which most of my illuminative insights have come to me. Developing the eyes to see and the ears to hear these insights is the work of the pilgrim. For me, illuminations in the form of an inner knowing or an influential dream prove more challenging to recognize and trust.

GIFTS OF CLARITY AND INSIGHT

Many times on my pilgrimage through life I could not see the way to proceed. On one of those occasions, I experienced an illumination through an inner knowing. My inner and outer resources had been depleted, and I had nothing to draw upon except the faith of others. A good friend brought me a box of crayons; I used them to draw in my journal. I created a child-like image of myself filled with the light of God. It was a simple line drawing shaped like a gingerbread woman, which I filled with bright yellow color to represent the light of Christ. As I finished the drawing—and not a second before—I knew I would survive the confusion. A way would open, though I did not know when. It was a quiet, inner knowing and nothing more. There were no angelic choirs or golden lights, except for the golden yellow of the crayon in the drawing. I was given exactly what I needed.

Illuminations are pure grace, which no amount of striving will achieve. They come to the pilgrim in God's time, just as a creative insight comes to the artist, and it takes wisdom to recognize them when they occur. Illuminations of grace are always absolutely specific to the pilgrim's need; they bring healing and courage to continue on the path. These gifts of clarity and insight move the pilgrim deeper and deeper, spawning a more intimate relationship with the Divine Lover. Sometimes illuminations visit us at the center of meditation and prayer as God shines light on our path and in our hearts, but they can come at any time, in any place, and through any means—even a yellow crayon. They often answer our deepest, most heartfelt prayers. These may be prayers we do not even know we have prayed or prayers that wait unarticulated in a recessed chamber of our heart. Our deepest prayers—the prayers of our soul—often remain unknown to us until they are answered. When experiencing an illumination on the pilgrim's journey, we know we have received an answer to our prayer from the God who is the Keeper of Promises and the Giver of Every Good Gift.

Exercise

A Way of Seeing

*Either you see God in Everything or you have lost the
basis for seeing God in Anything.*

—RICHARD ROHR[3]

MATERIALS NEEDED
*18" x 24" drawing paper
crayons or colorful markers*

In the fifth grade I got my first pair of glasses; when I put
them on I was amazed to see leaves on trees. I gazed at trees
outside the classroom window every chance I got. The leaves
were beautiful, and I enjoyed looking at their shape. They
were much prettier than the fuzzy globs of green atop brown
stem I had seen before. Seeing takes time and practice, and
sometimes we need new lenses on our eyes to see clearly.
Seeing through the eyes of Love reveals the world as a beautiful place where all God's children are lovely.

Ask the God of Creation to give you the eyes of Divine
Love during this exercise and to guide you through it. Look at
an ordinary houseplant or a small outdoor shrub from the distance of ten feet. Really look at it. What do you see? Move five
feet closer. What do you see now? Move close enough to touch
the plant. Examine the plant and study it from this close perspective. What do you observe now that you did not perceive
from the distance of ten feet?

Using crayons or colorful markers, draw the plant. Your
drawing does not have to be an exact replica of the plant.
Draw what you felt or observed about the plant as your

perspective changed. Your drawing might display only one leaf or blossom. It might be an impression of the colors you noticed in the plant. When you finish, ask yourself if the plant looks different to you.

Seeing takes time for both the artist and the pilgrim. To see the world, our neighbor, and ourselves as God sees us is an art to be practiced.

The Emerging True Self

When you are invited by someone to a wedding banquet, do not sit down at the place of honor, in case someone more distinguished than you has been invited by your host; and the host who invited both of you may come and say to you, "Give this person your place," and then in disgrace you would start to take the lowest place. But when you are invited, go and sit down at the lowest place, so that when your host comes, he may say to you, "Friend, move up higher"; then you will be honored in the presence of all who sit at the table with you. For all who exalt themselves will be humbled, and those who humble themselves will be exalted.

—LUKE 14:8-11

As an artist, I respond to the gift of insight in the illumination stage with obedience. This long-sought-after gift carries me deeper into creativity. My obedience comes not as rigid response made out of fear, the way a frightened dog obeys a cruel master; rather, this obedience is generated out of love and gratitude for the chance to work at my craft in this lifetime. It flows from a full heart, not a contracted one. Most working artists are extremely grateful to be using their talent. They gladly obey the creative urge for the chance to do what they love.

CREATIVE ILLUMINATION AS A CALL

A creative insight, whispered into the heart of the artist at this stage, causes the creative process to feel spiritual, even slightly mystical. Though scientists inform us that these breakthroughs are related to levels of nitric oxide in the body, they still cannot explain the source of the insight and the reason it is specific to the artist's need. Those matters remain a mystery. Perhaps it is this mysterious specificity that makes the artist feel chosen to express the insight in the world. Much as God chose Esther "for just such a time as this," the Creator chooses artists to contribute their gifts, shaping the world into a more beautiful and loving place.

Each time I am chosen to receive a precious "Aha!" moment, I am awed and sometimes overwhelmed at the responsibility to manifest this insight in the world. A lifetime of being chosen might lead me to become self-righteous and arrogant, like a misguided mystic who believes God's special graces grant special privileges. However, if artists come to this work through obedience and a grateful heart, they know being chosen simply makes them a servant of the work.

GRATITUDE AND HUMILITY

A grateful heart reminds artists they do not deserve an illumination, even though they may long for it. They do not deserve it in that they did not earn it. Given as God's grace is given— freely and unconditionally—an illumination comes to the artist like life itself. It comes because artists are loved and cherished, as all are loved, by a God who adores creativity.

It is humbling for artists to realize that though they did not earn the illumination, they are at its mercy. Without it, the creative process cannot continue. Like beggars who receive an invitation to a royal banquet, artists who welcome the "Aha!" moment feast sumptuously at their craft. Such a gift engenders gratitude in the heart of an artist.

Humility and gratitude form two sides of the same coin. Humility comes from knowing you have been invited to the banquet where others far more worthy than you sit at the table. Realizing your limitations and being allowed to do what you love anyway fosters this virtue.

Humility differs from low self-esteem. Thinking you have nothing to offer and suffering from an inferiority complex characterize false humility. True humility does not imply we have no self; rather, it leads us to be unself-conscious. Real humility requires a strong, positive sense of self, and only the courageous, who have forged a good self-image out of the raw material of their lives, can possess it. A truly humble person acknowledges strengths as well as weaknesses and accepts both as integral parts of the self without judgment or egotistical pride.

The humble do not need to sit at the head table but are simply grateful to be at the banquet. Unfortunately, this virtue often comes through loss, the kind of loss that teaches us we are vulnerable as well as strong.

WEARING DOWN SHARP EDGES

Loss has a way of humbling even the most arrogant. It connects us to our own fragility and to one another. None of us can get through life without loss; it is part of being human. The longer we live, the greater number of losses we will suffer. If we live long enough, we lose our flexibility and mobility; our hearing and sight fade; and the number of our friends and family dwindles as they pass through death's door. Aging provides us with plenty of opportunity to learn about loss.

As a child my sheltered upbringing brought few losses out of the ordinary. In my late twenties I began to deal with loss in ways that shape you. I failed miserably in my first career as a parish pastor. I had invested four years and a large sum of money in graduate school to prepare for a life of service in local congregations. Full of hope and the enthusiasm of youth, I ran into roadblocks made up of individuals who did not want a liberal, creative woman pastor. I could do nothing to persuade them otherwise. It did not matter how well crafted my sermons were or how many hospital visits I made. They did not want me in the role of their pastor because of qualities I could not change about myself, elements integral to who God created me to be. At the time, their rejection came as a crushing blow.

Before that experience of loss, I thought I understood life: all difficulties could be resolved through conversation and reason. After my sharp edges had been worn down in the struggle, I knew I did not understand much at all. My close friends told me the failure had changed me for the better. I was easier to be around, less judgmental, and much less arrogant. Loss softens us and connects us to our vulnerability.

Unless we are born with a predisposition for humility, it does not often characterize the very young. The young are busy accumulating skills and possessions. Out of necessity, they are testing their limits and discovering their strengths. Only as we mature does humility have an opportunity to germinate within us. If we live long enough to suffer a few losses, hopefully we will grow to accept our weaknesses, our vulnerability, and our limitations. Loss helps the pilgrim take a humble place alongside the rest of the human family. It knits us together in one fabric.

Loss as a Door to Gratitude

Potentially loss can open our hearts to gratitude. As a teen I spent months recuperating from a severe case of hepatitis. I ventured outside my bedroom only on trips to the doctor's office. After multiple weeks in bed, I was glad to be going anywhere, even to the doctor. On one of my first trips I was overwhelmed by the exquisite beauty of the green grass and trees; it almost hurt to look at them. Before my illness I had not noticed trees and grass coming in so many shades of green or being so beautiful. Grateful to see the lush variety of spring greens and to breathe in their earthy fragrance, I soaked up the experience like our black dog soaks up the sun. As my strength was returning, I painted a picture to capture my gratitude for the beauty of that moment. In half-hour sessions I stood before the canvas applying color and then, exhausted, returned to bed to sleep for hours. Though I do not want to relive that illness, I would not give up the experience captured in the painting for a golden monkey.

Pilgrims who have come through the dark night into the dawn often say they would not trade their experiences for anything, but neither would they choose to relive them. The dark night makes pilgrims aware of their vulnerability, of God's greatness, and of their reliance upon divine mercy for everything they have and all they do.

A French prayer I learned expresses this realization well: "God, my boat is very small and your ocean is very large. Carry me home." The awareness of our limitations and our needs comes to us as our true self emerges during the illumination period of the pilgrim's journey.

Only with hindsight do we have true sight regarding how the losses of the dark night shape us. In the dawn we meet our truest self, seeing with gratitude—perhaps for the first time—how God cradles us in mercy and carries us home on an ocean of love. Our reliance upon divine mercy tends to generate humility in the heart of the pilgrim.

Humility, which often blooms with the authentic self, makes love and acceptance possible. It equips us as pilgrims to love as Christ loved by accepting others where they are and loving them with all their faults. The humbled true self also enables us to love and accept ourselves just as we are, warts and all. Humility happens when we realize we are loved without qualification or condition. This kind of love produces a compassionate heart toward oneself and others.

Experiencing life through the eyes of humility binds us to one another and frees us from needing to be center stage. It allows us to become servants who humbly, and with a grateful heart, carry out God's work of love in the world.

Exercise

Thank You

Thanksgiving is a gesture of the whole heart,
or it is nothing.

—Brother David Steindl-Rast[4]

MATERIALS NEEDED
18" x 24" paper
old magazines
scissors
glue stick or white glue
colorful markers

A guest in our home gave my spouse and me a card that read, "Gratitude is an attitude of the heart." Gratitude, like humility, cannot be generated by our efforts alone; the Divine is the source of both qualities. We can, however, practice gratitude like a spiritual discipline, making room for God to foster this attitude in our life. Gratitude grows in our hearts as a seed planted by God. Though the Divine is the source of both the seed and its growth, we can nurture this quality.

For years I kept a gratitude journal in which I counted my blessings on a daily basis. The practice taught me to see as gifts much that I habitually had taken for granted. I found the more I said thank-you, the more occasions I had to be grateful. My gratitude, which was the size of a mustard seed in the beginning, grew more encompassing of all life in a matter of time. This discipline was particularly helpful during the difficult and dark times. It changed my attitude and gave me a lighter heart.

In this exercise you are invited to make a gratitude collage. Remember to invite the Giver of All Good Gifts to guide you. You may want to write a title on top of a large sheet of paper in colorful markers. My collage is titled "God Is Great. God Is Good." Create a title appropriate to your life. Using old magazines, tear or cut images that represent items, qualities, or people for which you are grateful today. Arrange these pictures on a large sheet of paper. The images do not have to represent big-ticket items; they can represent things like the shower you took this morning or the cookie you had at lunch. You decide which images belong in your collage.

Once you have filled the page, begin to glue or paste the images onto the paper. A glue stick is the simplest way to fix them to the page, but slightly diluted white glue also works well. Covering the entire back surface of the image with glue will help keep it in place.

When finished, place your gratitude collage where you can see it every day. Look at it each day for a week, mentally noting what you would like to add to the collage. When new things come to mind for which you are grateful, simply say a quiet thank-you.

You can repeat this exercise periodically in your life. The collages become a way to examine how you have changed over the months and years.

Elaboration

Cleaning Toilets

*Not that I have already obtained this or have already
reached the goal; but I press on to make it my own,
because Christ Jesus has made me his own.*

—PHILIPPIANS 3:12

Whoever described creativity as 10 percent inspiration and
90 percent perspiration is right. The elaboration stage, the
final phase of the creative process, deals with the sweat. Artists,
often relieved to receive the gift of an illumination, sometimes mistakenly think the creative insight is the end of the
process. It is not; there is still much work to do—about 90 percent of the work.

In the elaboration stage, artists get their hands dirty. The
painter applies paint to canvas; the choreographer works out
new steps; the composer blends instruments to achieve the
perfect sound; and the quilter painstakingly stitches thread
into a design on fabric. Without these concrete acts of flesh-
ing out the inspiration, the "Aha!" moment becomes a dying
ideal. The elaboration stage comprises the hands-on work
that manifests a piece of art in the world.

GETTING PHYSICAL

Creativity is very physical. I am particularly aware of this as I
age. I used to think nothing of working on a ten-foot canvas,
but now my knees and hips hurt at the end of each day from

all the bending and stretching. Even the act of writing requires sitting in the same chair for hours at a time, which makes my aging muscles and joints complain loudly. It takes a great deal of hard physical labor to move a brilliant insight from the point of inspiration into a concrete, tangible form like a painting, a book, or a piece of sculpture.

The creative process moves from the ethereal to the earthy in the elaboration stage. An idea has to be embodied in an artistic medium before the insight can affect the world. Similarly, the Creator's love had to be embodied in creation and in the person of Jesus before the world could know the extent of divine love. Creative energy—the gift of God's loving self, the gift of God's Word—must take on form to be realized. In this respect creativity is incarnational.

Love always extends itself on behalf of others, or it is not love but sentimentality. Creativity as an expression of love must be used in service of others. Like love, creativity needs to extend itself beyond the one in whom it is embodied. Without the drive to express, creativity remains incomplete and impotent. Creativity, like love, must offer itself as a gift for others to be authentic.

GETTING STUCK

Artists make great "idea people"; they love playing with new concepts. If artists become stymied at this stage, they may lack the energy or drive to bring an idea into a physical form, preferring inspiration over sweat. No matter what the medium, artists enjoy certain aspects of their work better than others. The monotony in the elaboration stage may be wearisome for some artists. For instance, the drab process of priming multiple canvases feels like death to me. It stops me in my tracks because it seems unimaginative. Surprisingly, many parts of the creative process can be tedious. Painters have to mix paint and stretch canvases; musicians have to practice, practice, practice; and writers have to craft a book word by word, sitting at the same computer day after day after day.

The actual nuts and bolts of creativity are often unexciting and anticlimactic when compared to a dramatic illumination. Having to construct a physical form from a cherished insight can be perceived as almost superfluous to the creative thinking in which the artist has been engaged. To the artist who has meditated upon the insight and mentally executed it with numerous and lovely details it may seem that the real work has been done. For those who delight in new ideas, working with an idea that has been chewed on for a while can be awfully tiresome. At times in the life of an artist it takes sheer grit and tenacity to bring a piece of art through the elaboration stage to a conclusion. When I am in this frame of mind, it can feel like I am cleaning toilets.

Love Transforms

One of my friends visits his aging aunt in an assisted living center weekly. His aunt suffers from the beginnings of dementia, poor vision, and a mild form of incontinence. Near the end of each visit, my friend cleans the toilet. The bathroom, though scoured weekly, occasionally needs more attention than the staff can give it. My friend does not enjoy the task. It is messy and monotonous, but he does it out of love for his aunt. Most often, my friend cleans the toilet out of pure determination, but once in a while, it takes no effort at all. His love for his aunt makes this simple act of service possible. Love transforms even the most tedious tasks by giving them meaning.

Love motivates many actions, from cleaning toilets to finishing a work of art. If the artist loves a creative idea into existence and loves the process too, the task of creating can be effortless. However, if the process becomes tedious, artists pray love will provide strength and determination to persevere.

When I am merely persisting in the elaboration stage, I remind myself of the wonderful sensation of having a finished work of art to show for my labor. It is similar to having a clean bathroom, only better. If holding the hope of the end goal does not help me stay the course, I promise myself chocolate ice cream at the end of the day for sticking with the job at hand. Cultivating a lasting friendship with delayed gratification equips the artist with an essential tool for accomplishing less-than-favorite tasks in the creative process.

AN INVITATION TO CONTINUE

The pilgrim's temptation to cease journeying resembles the temptation that lures the artist from completing a work of art. An artist savoring a dramatic creative breakthrough may linger too long with the illumination, losing momentum on the project. The same stumbling block applies to the pilgrim who mistakenly believes a divine illumination is the end of the road and that life will be smooth sailing from that point on. As pilgrims who have moved from the dark night to a more emotionally open and free space, we desire to stay a while in the good feelings, to construct tents on the mountaintop and set up camp. However, the illuminating insight signals the beginning of another phase of the journey toward divine union; more work lies ahead for the pilgrim. An illumination in the life of the pilgrim is not an invitation to cease traveling but an enticement to break camp and continue on down the spiritual path.

This familiar story from Zen Buddhism describes the invitation of the illumination and elaboration stages well. A disciple, upon reaching enlightenment, calls out to his teacher, "Master, I've been enlightened! What do I do now?!" Wisely the master responds to his student, "Fetch water and chop wood," the same duties the disciple performed before his enlightenment. I love this story because it teaches us to continue on the inner road after a divine illumination no matter how wonderful our experience might have been. The story also informs us that much of the work following our religious experience may be similar to what we did before our illumination, even the work we previously found to be monotonous and boring.

Not many of us are able to avoid cleaning toilets in this life; we all have necessary though uninspiring and even tedious tasks on the spiritual journey. We may find it an effort to keep a daily prayer time, to attend weekly worship, to volunteer in a soup kitchen, or to do the children's laundry. People in our lives may tax our patience or try our loving Christian nature. An illumination in the spiritual life, rather than making us more ethereal and taking us away from the daily grind, causes us to be more earthy and more fully involved in life's day-to-day activities. It brings us face-to-face with the children's dirty laundry, our difficulty with a disciplined prayer life, and the person who tries our patience. We may deeply desire to pray all day, but God—and life—have different plans for us. Meals must be cooked; dogs must be walked; and deadlines must be met.

An Icon of God

As we incarnate God's new energies of love—from our cell tissue to our energy field—we become more fully human, the way Jesus was human. We grow into the brightest and best we can be. Incorporating greater degrees of divine love in our being brings forth our true self and leads us to the place of our own resurrection. Who we are meant to be shines forth for all to see, unfettered by the false self and its attachments. As the false self dies, we are more ourselves than we have ever been. Each of us, shaped into an icon of God, becomes a transparent window to the Divine. Others now see God in and through us more clearly than they did before.

Through death of the false self and resurrection of the true self, we build the New Jerusalem on earth, even as we are a part of it. At this place on the spiritual journey, who we are as much as what we do helps to usher in the new heaven and new earth. Whether walking down the street or building homes for the homeless, we embody God's love as it radiates forth from within us. This presence of love changes the world.

Occasionally an illumination dramatically alters our outer life, causing us to change jobs or even friends, but most of the time an illumination causes an interior shift. More often than not, we find ourselves cleaning the same toilets we did before the dark night and its resulting illumination— with one major difference. We do everything with greater love because we are more loving. Though our lives may look no different, in reality everything has changed. Love has given us a radically different motivation for doing the work God puts in our path. Our perspective shifts from a self-centered motivation to a deeper desire to love God, neighbor, and self. We move from *What's in it for me?* to *How can I be more loving as God's servant?*

At this point on the journey, pilgrims may grow in awareness that the gifts of illumination are not just for personal benefit. Though we are the first to receive the gifts, they flow through us for the good of God's creation. Since receiving a new sense of peace at the time of my heartwarming experience, people comment on the peace and calm they experience in my presence. They feel God's peace, not mine. God's gifts may feed the recipient first, but the recipient then feeds others. God is our original, renewable energy source!

GIFTS BECOME WORK

The gifts of the dark night revealed in the subsequent illumination become the pilgrim's focus in the elaboration stage. Like an artist learning to work with a new medium, we pilgrims have to learn how to use our new gifts to benefit all God's creation. Living with deeper love for God's world radically changes our perception of life. Given eyes to see and ears to hear, we live from the perspective of love. This perspective on life, while a marvelous gift, also becomes tremendous work. If any residue of the false self remains, it will want to take credit for the gifts we have received. Spiritual pride, one of the seven deadly sins, can impede the pilgrim's journey.

Following a divine illumination, we may experience a desire to change a habit or reinforce another. Shortly after my divine surprise, I realized my thinking had grown negative and fearful. I began a discipline to change my negative thinking by treating it like the addiction it is. I was not motivated by perfectionism or works righteousness, as I might have been prior to the dark night; my motivation was—and is—love. Through a process of surrendering the negative thought and replacing it with a positive one, I am slowly making progress. After my dark night, I know my negative thoughts already have been conquered by Love. All I must do is change my habits. This takes conscious and continuous work.

At the end of each day, I examine the places where I have experienced God, focusing particularly on the transformation of my thought patterns. Occasionally I discover I have had no negative thoughts; these days are grace-filled. However, on many days it seems all I have done is surrendered the negativity. On these days I feel like I'm still cleaning toilets. The difference is that I do not mind the work the way I did before the dark night. Now I know in my marrow that Love already has won the battle with my false self, and I am being transformed into a beautiful work of art. Love makes all things possible.

Exercise

Here We Go Again

> *There is always strength for struggle. The sure knowledge of the fact gives wings to the spirit even when the struggle is deepest.*
>
> —Howard Thurman[1]

MATERIALS NEEDED

8 ½" x 11" paper
pie pan or template
crayons and markers

Much of my life has seemed like a struggle. I have struggled to incorporate exercise and a healthy diet; I have wrestled with scheduling regular prayer time; I have labored to create wholesome relationships. With my dark night came a lessening of the struggle. Those areas of my life still take work, but the striving has been replaced with loving.

Struggling without the assurance of being on the right path actually created room for more Love in my life. The struggle is important. Those times when it takes all our strength to put one foot in front of the other shape us. In the search for the place of our resurrection these periods of difficulty become highly significant.

In the section titled "Preparation," you made a mandala. You will make another one in this exercise. Ask the Holy Creative Spirit to guide you.

Draw a circle with a circumference that takes in almost the entire page. Use a dinner plate or a pie pan as a template if you wish. Combine markers and crayons to fill the circle with color. Prayerfully represent what is going on in your life right now that makes you feel like you are cleaning toilets. Where is the struggle for you? What form does it take? If you face no current struggle, draw a former one.

Do not try to represent images unless it feels appropriate to do so. Many mandalas consist only of color and pattern. Create as you feel led.

No Proof, Only Trust

Many who are first will be last, and the last will be first.

—MATTHEW 19:30

An artist told me that holding the promise of a beautifully finished piece of art before his mind's eye motivates him. However, if he goes any further into the future to picture the imagined success or failure of his art, the road gets rocky. He loses his focus as well as his creativity. My friend said this happens every time he carries the vision too far. Familiarity with this pitfall should be enough to keep his mind in present time, but it is not. He confessed to being like a child who cannot avoid picking at a scab; he plays the "what if" game all the time. "What if this current project is an enormous success?" and "What if no one likes it?" "What if it sells?" and "What if it doesn't?" In vivid detail, he thinks his way into a state of anxiety or depression within a matter of minutes. The "what if" game is a short road to insanity, and it is a very quick trip.

STAY IN THE MOMENT

When I am tempted to "what if" my way into the future, my creativity trails my imagination into a land of make-believe. If I catch myself, I can hear the wise words of my mentor in my head: "Do the work; just do the work." The words come like a life preserver thrown to me as I start to sink into my own sea of emotions. On good days I make a conscious choice to follow her advice, leaving behind concerns over which I have little or no control. "Focus on the work," I tell myself, "the rest will take care of itself. Stay in the moment. Now is the only time I have." I repeat this like a mantra as I come back to the labor of creativity. Trusting all will be well or momentarily deciding not to think about the future success or failure of my creation, I return to the present. The challenge becomes finding a way to stay in the moment. When I am in a good mood, enjoying my work, this is a piece of cake. On bad days, when I would rather be doing anything but the work before me, staying in the moment seems nearly impossible.

One such day I was on my hands and knees painting a sprawling, twelve-foot banner. My knees ached, and I wearied of my chosen paint color. My mind began to skip down that rocky path into the future. *What does success look like?* I wondered. *Is it when my work is viewed by an audience of thousands instead of hundreds?* The image of throngs of people "oohing" and "aahing" over my work hooked me. My desire for success had me by the throat. With my creativity ebbing, I knew I had better do something fast before this fantasy did its disastrous deed. I knocked off work for the evening in hopes of a better tomorrow.

Don't Look Them in the Eyes

Turning my attention to daily-living chores, I picked up the cleaning and did the grocery shopping. When I change my focus to such tasks, sometimes the "what ifs" are subverted. If that does not work, I try arduous physical exercise or prayer. Both these activities can be done only in present time. They keep me grounded in the moment.

As an artist and a pilgrim, I never win in a face-to-face battle with my insecurities. They have power over me that only grows stronger when I look into their eyes.

Sometimes I have to trick my self-doubts into going away by pretending I am uninterested, that these insecurities rate lower than the dry cleaning on my fascination scale. If trickery fails, there is always prayer, which is probably already at work within me as I pick up the laundry. In either case, a Power greater than myself works to free me from all that holds me captive, including my insecurities.

FAITHFULNESS IS THE GOAL

That evening, after completing the chores, I retired, looking forward to eight hours without the "what ifs." I had a most illuminating dream. In the dream I worked behind the stage at a large conference, attending to the details of making the event run smoothly. As the conference began, the speakers were introduced with great fanfare and applause. To my surprise, the announcer introduced me next as the person who had made the visuals for the auditorium and done most of the grunt work for the conference. The audience went wild with applause, clapping, cheering, and jumping to their feet. I was getting ready to take a bow when I looked over my shoulder to see Mother Teresa, humbly standing in the wings behind the curtain. Waking up from the dream with a chuckle, I laughed out loud at myself for the frivolous thoughts of success I had the previous day.

The dream reminded me of the importance of being faithful to the work the way Mother Teresa was faithful to her work. She cared for one person at a time out of her love for Christ with no thought given to success or worldwide acclaim.

Doing the work, simply doing the work, is all that God calls any of us to do: one brushstroke, one word at a time, with no attention given to the outcome. Future success is not the goal; faithfulness in the moment is.

INSECURITIES

I remember as a teen saying to my mother, "I just want to be popular," when what I truly wanted was a shortcut to self-acceptance. I think my "what if" game, my hopes of success and fears of failure, is rooted in the same longing, though clothed in a more age-appropriate disguise. The desire for success comes from that same place deep inside me that cried out for popularity in my youth. Self-acceptance, like self-love, is a lifelong process. My insecurities pull me away from present time into a fantasy future, but I cannot create in the future. I can make art only in the moment.

My Mother Teresa dream points out another insecurity. I worry that my artistic calling is insignificant in the grand scheme of things. I look at those who shelter the homeless and feed the hungry, those who work in the political arena to create just laws, and those in the medical field who heal bodies and emotions; and I ask myself, "Of what importance is this painting or that book in comparison to all the needs facing our world?" A fear gnaws at me that my life's calling is trivial and will not change the world for the better. I have dismissed this calling again and again as unimportant, yearning to be someone I am not, doing something I am not called to do. I have thought of my artistic leanings as something to do in my retirement after I have had a "real job" for thirty-five years. I have wondered if I would have a more positive impact on the world if I were a little more like Florence Nightingale or

Hillary Clinton or Sojourner Truth. Then I remember the Mother Teresa dream. The audience was clapping for me and for the work I had done. Though I may fear my work holds no significance in the grand scheme of things, my dream gives me hope the work contains meaning beyond my experience of it.

THE ARTIST'S CALL

As an artist and writer, I am called to create truthful expressions of beauty and to contemplate the meaning of life's events. Beauty, the original soul food, nourishes us in our parched places. It sustains us in our difficulties and restores a lighthearted joy to our spirit. Contemplation helps excavate meaning from life's common and uncommon events. It connects our story to the stories of others and the larger faith story. When we search for the place of our own resurrection we search for meaning, and none of us can find meaning without soul food, sustenance, and the stories of others. Instead of worrying about the merit of my calling as an artist, I really need to treasure this priceless gift I have been given, boldly remain faithful to the work, and stay in the present moment. God will take care of the outcome.

IS THIS ALL THERE IS?

Insecurity about living a significant life is not solely the property of artists. Spiritual pilgrims suffer from self-doubts too. Trappist monk Thomas Merton confessed in his "prayer of trust" an uncertainty about pleasing God with his life's choices. In the same prayer, Merton simultaneously affirmed the ability of divine grace to lead him by the road of God's choosing though he may never know how he fits into the divine plan. If a monk can suffer from these insecurities, I guess the rest of us pilgrims can too.

Life's routine nature makes those who endeavor to be faithful pilgrims question, "Are we on the right path? Is this all there is?" Going to the office each day; making beds; washing cars, children, and clothes; and completing tasks for which we may lack enthusiasm give us pause. Are we contributing to a bigger picture, a divine plan? The truth is we may never know on this side of the veil. Though we may desire to do what pleases God, many of us have no earthly idea what that is. Rarely do we receive divine confirmation we are actually doing what God intends for our lives.

It Is Still about Trust

If we pilgrims use success as a yardstick to measure our compliance with God's yearning for our lives, we have to come to terms with Jesus' life. By worldly standards he was an utter failure. Success holds no proof we are cooperating with the Creator's desire for us. I've known those who have left successful jobs with good salaries to follow a perceived calling into a career paying next to nothing and offering little public acclaim. Success and public recognition offer no guarantees we have found the right path.

A wise woman once told me we are most effective as God's servants when we are least aware of having any effect at all. In other words, it is a matter of trust. We never get away from needing to exercise trust and faith on the spiritual journey. Even after a dark night and divine illumination, our faith plays a critical role on our pilgrim path.

We may never see the results of our life's labor, but we trust that God does see. Unbeknownst to us, the Divine Lover will find ways to use our meager and often mundane offerings to build up the reign of Love on earth. Our task is to stay in the moment and do the work of each day. For that we need trust.

Exercise

Ordering the Day

Success is being freed from the inside by a self-acceptance which releases the energies of rebirth within us.

—ROBERT RAINES[2]

MATERIALS NEEDED
your calendar
18" x 24" paper
tempera paints
paintbrush
container for water
paint rag

In my thirties I began asking God to make order out of my chaotic calendar, with amazing results. I continue this practice today. In the morning, as an act of trust, I release my plans for the day. I trust the Divine knows what must be accomplished. I ask the Holy One to use me to bring about a reign of Love, even though I may know nothing about how that occurs. Some days, appointments unexpectedly cancel; uninvited visitors show up; and I find I am in the right place at the right time. Other days, my schedule remains unchanged from my previous planning.

In this exercise you are invited to surrender the next few minutes to the Great Creator. Let your imagination carry you to where you are most yourself and closest to God. With your calendar in hand, ask the Divine One to help bring order to this day and this week. Spend a few moments looking at the appointments on your calendar. If there are none, think about the tasks you need to accomplish over the next twenty-four hours and over the next week. If it feels comfortable, surrender the tasks and the appointments, allowing God to work within them.

When you have completed this act of trust, paint what it felt like to invite God into your calendar. Remember you do not have to make your picture look like anything. It can simply be colors or lines. You are attempting to draw the feeling or sensation of surrendering the day.

If you feel stuck or are having difficulty with your painting, try using your nondominant hand to paint. When finished, examine the painting for clues to emotions of which you may be unaware. What does this painting tell you about yourself? What does it tell you about God?

A Small Death

*Very truly, I tell you, unless a grain of wheat falls into
the earth and dies, it remains just a single grain; but
if it dies, it bears much fruit.*

—JOHN 12:24

Making art holds birth and death in close proximity. I was
almost ready to give birth to a creative project I had yearned
to do for nearly a decade. At that point I confessed to another
artist that I thought I might die when the work was completed. The feelings seemed completely irrational, but that
assessment did not make them go away or make me want to
finish the work anytime soon. The other artist, kindly addressing my fears, replied, "All artists feel that way. We either fear
we will die or that we will never, ever create anything else
again, which is also a kind of death."

Just as the pilgrim in the middle of a dark night of the soul
wonders whether the experience marks the death of the false
self or the birth of the true self, the artist struggles to distin-
guish between birth and death while in the middle of the creative process. Sometimes the creative process leads the artist
to give birth to new aspects of personality. At other times,
parts of the artist seem to be dying a painful death. The veil
becomes more sheer than we like to think in these life-and-
death experiences.

GIVING BIRTH

Artists give birth to creations out of their thoughts, emotions, perceptions, time, talent, spirit, and soul; even their bodies have labored to turn creative energy into something tangible. Their creations express the deepest part of who they are, brought forth into the world. When I create, I am changed by what I create. Fresh nuances about my relationship to the Divine and the world come to me in the creative process, revealing new understandings of the truth of my existence.

As an artist my feelings toward my artwork mirror the best feelings a parent can have for a child. I feel tender toward it, amazed by it, proud, and even humbled that such a thing could emerge from my being. I want to protect my creations (and myself) from criticism. However, the only way to protect my art is to keep it to myself, refusing to share it with others. Because the final part of the elaboration stage involves sharing the created work with the world, hiding art from public view curtails the creative process. My seminary professor understood this truth when he told our class, "A sermon isn't finished until it's preached. It may be written by Wednesday, but until it is delivered on Sunday morning, it isn't done." The completion of the creative process takes place in communicating the work of art with the world.

DYING

Once an artist has finished a pristine work of art, he or she must send the freshly birthed work into the world to stand on its own. No good parent would do this to a newborn child, but artists must send forth creations that feel much like their offspring. Every bit of the artist embodied in the artwork—heart, soul, body, and mind—now goes out to face the public. This is all well and good and as it should be. But it is terrifying. When the last bit of paint is brushed onto the canvas or the clay vessel enters the kiln for the final firing, the artist may feel as if she or he is the one who has stepped into the refining fire.

Exposing one's innermost thoughts and emotions to the public for their critique can make a person as vulnerable as the underbelly of a dog. This natural part of the creative process leaves the artist defenseless and unprotected. Sharing private information in a public arena can be a kind of death. The ego's preoccupation with itself begins to die in the face of public criticism. Like standing naked in Times Square during rush hour, the death of self-preoccupation is excruciating.

In order for artists to survive sending new creations out into the public, without cutting off an ear, they must relinquish attachment to their work of art. They have to disengage their ego from the work, no longer caring how the art will be received.

At this juncture I tell myself the piece of finished art no longer belongs to me. It belongs to the world; and the world will receive it or not as it chooses. I can do nothing short of locking my art in a closet, which would be a personal tragedy and an action I have no right to take. I have been given a gift, and like all gifts, it is not to be hoarded but shared. I tell myself this, but it takes a while for my feelings to catch up to my thinking.

Making art without putting oneself into the piece remains an impossibility. The more of the artist that goes into the work, the more the art birthed into the world resembles the artist, and the greater the loss when the art is released for public viewing. This releasing feels like an emptying, the way grief empties. Letting go of the work hollows out the artist and makes more space for creativity to thrive. Grief—though not always pronounced—claims its place as part of the creative process because loss is part of the process.

Every time I create, I learn a little about birth, loss, death, and grief. The cycle of creativity echoes the cycle of life—from birth to death through grief and back to birth again. If there were a way to avoid the feelings of loss and the resulting inner grief work in the artistic calling, I would have found it by now. I have searched and come up empty.

The Path to Servanthood

The creative process requires doing one's inner work, especially learning how to move through the accompanying loss and grief. I know an actor who intentionally leaves time between productions so that he can let go of his previous role and the investment of himself in it. He grieves the loss of the character he will no longer play. This kind of inner work around grieving gives him a plethora of rich material to take into the next expression of his artistic calling. His inner work with his emotions becomes fodder for creativity.

Rejections represent another kind of loss; they feel like a kind of small death. Artists must learn to deal with the rejection that comes in sharing their work with the world. Not everyone will like the art or consider the artist a creative genius. Rejections come with the territory, and they help shape the artist, every bit as much as successes do—maybe more. Learning to deal with rejections takes experience and time. There is no easy way to learn how to accept them gracefully.

Like river water smoothing the stones in a riverbed over many years, grief, rejection, and loss wear away the ego's engrossment with itself. This process for artists compares to pilgrims' working out their own salvation (Phil. 2:12). In fear and trembling, artists, like pilgrims, must do their own inner emotional work. With large doses of grace, in a process that can feel like death, artists are transformed into servants of creativity.

DEATH AND REBIRTH

The spiritual pilgrim coming through an experience of the dark night also experiences a diminishment of the ego's preoccupation with self. As the false self dies, scales fall from the pilgrim's eyes, bringing a new awareness of others' needs. The grief and loss of the dark night have hollowed out the pilgrim, making more room for the presence of the Divine Lover and generating greater love for the presence of all God's children. Before the dark night, pilgrims experience their own needs as primary; however, with the ego's self-engrossment lessening, increasing compassion toward others takes center stage.

After one experience of the dark night, I remember coming to the startling realization *Life is not just about me any more.* Writing this now makes me aware of how self-focused I was and how grateful I am that some of that focus has been transformed. In the true meaning of repentance, I did an about-face, turning away from self-preoccupation toward service to others.

After my dark night of the soul, a deep desire to serve God by serving others began to gain strength within me; it was all I wanted to do. Prior to the dark night, my motivation in life was finding a way to use my gifts. Thankfully that desire has been replaced by a simple yearning to be of service to God in the world, however that might happen. Whether through large acts or small, when I am helping or serving others, I notice the presence of deep, abiding joy; and I give thanks. Though I have by no means perfected a life of service, I know God works in me, transforming me into a servant of Love.

Servants of Love

If the pilgrim's journey is to be authentic, the elaboration stage must include service toward others. Like creativity, God's love has to be shared to be real love. The pilgrim has the opportunity now to use the fruits gained in the dark night for the benefit of the community. The Giver of Gifts opens a way for gifts to be used in acts of service, no matter how small those offerings might be. Acts of love are never wasted; they all contribute to building the new heaven and new earth.

Paradoxically, when we as pilgrims on the journey use our gifts on behalf of others, we find we are more ourselves than we ever have been. Our authentic self radiates forth in acts of loving service, unrestrained by our false self. This newly found freedom into which we have been invited by the One Who Loves Us is the freedom to be our true self, held and treasured by the Divine Lover.

Our pilgrim journey to become the person God has always intended us to be has taken us through the death of the false self and the birth of our true self. It has required all of our creativity to remove the years of camouflage that hid our light from the world. Initiated by Love and undertaken for the sake of Love, our pilgrimage has transformed us into servants of Love. Our light now shines brilliantly into the world. And as it shines, we discover we have reached the place of our own resurrection.

Exercise
Refining Gold

*When through fiery trials thy pathways shall lie,
my grace, all-sufficient, shall be thy supply;
the flame shall not hurt thee; I only design
thy dross to consume, and thy gold to refine.*

—"How Firm a Foundation"[3]

MATERIALS NEEDED
*18" x 24" paper
tempera paints
paintbrush
container for water
paint rag*

We all have experiences of feeling like a new person. After a refreshing night's sleep, we awaken with that sensation. Recovering from a round of flu makes us feel new again. In dozens of little ways we understand what it is to feel like new.

Can you remember such a time? If not, use your imagination. What would it feel like to be new? What would be different about you? What would stay the same? What is God doing in you right now to bring about your transformation?

In this exercise you will paint a "new you." Using your imagination and your intuition, create an image of how God is shaping you. What will you look like after the gold within you is refined. Can you picture your true self?

When you finish, hang your painting where you can see it every day. Let it remind you of God's continuous transforming work in your life. Say a prayer of thanksgiving.

Epilogue

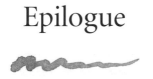

When we find the place of our own resurrection, we find the truth of our soul and the purpose for which we were born. This truth liberates us to live the unique and authentic life Love designed and kept safe for us until we were ready to embrace it. Though we remained unaware, God was at work transforming us on our pilgrim journey, preparing us to embody our soul's truth. Under the cover of darkness, deep in the mystery, the Holy One has readied us to receive the knowledge of our purpose in life.

In the place of our resurrection, as the purpose of our existence unfolds, a way opens to a life far richer and more expansive than we dared to dream. It is a life dripping with satisfaction and saturated with joy. Our revealed purpose may call us into our true vocation, what we are meant to do with our days; or it may manifest in an inward motivation for all we do and for how we live. Like the mystics, our "vocation" may become love. In any case, the place of our own resurrection is a place of unbounded freedom. Like Lazarus unfettered coming forth from the tomb, we step into the light of our new existence.

Finally free to dive headfirst into life, we pour our heart and soul into each twenty-four-hour gift, tasting every messy minute—both the pain and the joy. Holding nothing back, like children to whom the kingdom of God belongs, we embrace the depth and breadth of life in all its fierce beauty. We taste and see that life is good. In the deeper layers, in the place of our own resurrection, we savor the unshakable Love that is at the ground and center of it all.

It is this Love for which we have longed all our life, though we did not know it. It initiated our pilgrimage, though we were blind to it. This Love has been our rudder on the journey, though we could not sense it. This Love, which cannot be destroyed and from which we cannot be separated, has set us free, and we are born again into the wild joy of our own life— in the place of our own resurrection.

NOTES

PROLOGUE

1. Ann and Barry Ulanov, *Primary Speech: A Psychology of Prayer* (Atlanta: John Knox Press,1982), 2.

INVITATION

1. Esther De Waal, *The Celtic Way of Prayer* (New York: Doubleday, 1997), 2–3.
2. Phil Cousineau, *The Art of Pilgrimage: The Seeker's Guide to Making Travel Sacred* (Berkeley: Conari Press, 1998), 233.
3. Betty Edwards, *Drawing on the Right Side of the Brain: A Course in Enhancing Creativity and Artistic Confidence* (Los Angeles: J. P. Tarcher, 1979), 4.

ENCOUNTER

1. Rollo May, *The Courage to Create* (New York: Bantam Books, 1976), 39.
2. Ibid., 45.
3. Attributed to French Catholic novelist Leon Bloy, 1846–1917. Leon Bloy in a letter to Jacques Maritain.
4. Geoffrey Keynes, ed., *Blake's Complete Writings*, "Auguries of Innocence" (London: Oxford University Press, 1966), 431.
5. Marianne Williamson, *A Return to Love: Reflections on the Principles of A COURSE IN MIRACLES* (New York: HarperPerennial, 1993), 190–91.

6. "Service of Word and Table I," *The United Methodist Book of Worship* (Nashville: The United Methodist Publishing House, 1992), 36.

7. Lucia Capacchione, *The Power of Your Other Hand: A Course in Channeling the Inner Wisdom of the Right Brain* (North Hollywood, Calif.: Newcastle Publishing Co., Inc., 1988), 4–5.

8. From Letter T51 to Felice da Massa, Catherine of Siena, *The Letters of Catherine of Siena*, trans. Suzanne Noffke (Binghamton, N.Y.: Medieval and Renaissance Texts and Studies, 1988), 635.

9. Thomas Keating, *Invitation to Love: The Way of Christian Contemplation* (New York: Continuum, 2000), 8.

10. Meister Eckhart, *Meister Eckhart*, trans. C. De B. Evans (London: John M. Watkins, 1956), 1:59.

11. Nevin Compton Trammell, untitled. Unpublished poem.

PREPARATION

1. John S. Dacey and Kathleen H. Lennon, *Understanding Creativity: The Interplay of Biological, Psychological, and Social Factors* (San Francisco: Jossey-Bass Publishers, 1998), 34–35.

2. Rainer Maria Rilke, *Letters to a Young Poet*, rev. ed., trans. M. D. Herter Norton (New York: W. W. Norton & Company, 1954), 35.

3. Ibid., 30.

4. Richard J. Foster, *Celebration of Discipline: The Path to Spiritual Growth*, rev. ed. (San Francisco: Harper & Row Publishers, 1988), 7.

5. Henri J. M. Nouwen, *Making All Things New* (San Francisco: Harper & Row, 1981), 67.

6. Frederick Buechner, *Listening to Your Life*, ed. George Connor (San Francisco: HarperSanFrancisco, 1992), 2.

7. Henri J. M. Nouwen, *The Way of the Heart: Desert Spirituality and Contemporary Ministry* (New York: Seabury Press, 1981), 25.

8. Robert Frost, "The Road Not Taken," in *The Poetry of Robert Frost*, ed. Edward Connery Lathem (New York: Henry Holt and Company, 1979), 105.

9. Jim Forest, *Praying with Icons* (Maryknoll, N.Y.: Orbis Books, 1997), 35.

10. Benjamin Hoff, *The Tao of Pooh* (Middlesex, England: Penguin Books, 1982), 148.

11. Flora Slosson Wuellner, *Prayer, Stress, and Our Inner Wounds* (Nashville: Upper Room Books, 1985), 25.

FRUSTRATION

1. Friedrich Nietzsche, *Thus Spoke Zarathustra: A Book for All and None*, trans. Walter Kaufmann (New York: Modern Library, 1995), 17.

2. Inscription at Robert Kennedy's gravesite, Arlington Cemetery, by Aeschylus, third century BCE.

3. Henri J. M. Nouwen, *Behold the Beauty of the Lord: Praying with Icons* (Notre Dame, Ind.: Ave Maria Press, 1987), 19.

INCUBATION

1. Candace B. Pert, *Molecules of Emotion: Why You Feel the Way You Feel* (New York: Touchstone Books, 1999), 21.

2. Steve Garnaas-Holmes, "Somebody Loves Me Like a River," on *Take the Barriers Down* performed by Montana Logging and Ballet Company (recording). MLBC Publishing, 1987.

3. Frederick Buechner, *A Room Called Remember: Uncollected Pieces* (San Francisco: Harper & Row Publishers, 1984), 103.

4. Marjorie J. Thompson, *Soul Feast: An Invitation to the Christian Spiritual Life* (Louisville, Ky.: Westminster John Knox Press, 1995), 122.

5. "Service of Christian Marriage I," *The United Methodist Book of Worship* (Nashville: The United Methodist Publishing House, 1992), 127.

ILLUMINATION

1. Gerald G. May, *The Dark Night of the Soul: A Psychiatrist Explores the Connection Between Darkness and Spiritual Growth* (San Francisco: HarperSanFrancisco, 2004), 133.

2. Oswald Chambers, *My Utmost for His Highest: Selections for the Year* (New York: Dodd, Mead & Company, 1935), 25.

3. Richard Rohr, *Hope Against Darkness: The Transforming Vision of Saint Francis in an Age of Anxiety* (Cincinnati, Ohio: St. Anthony Messenger Press, 2001), 70.

4. Brother David Steindl-Rast, *Gratefulness, the Heart of Prayer: An Approach to Life in Fullness* (New York: Paulist Press, 1984), 19.

ELABORATION

1. Howard Thurman, *Meditations of the Heart* (Boston: Beacon Press, 1953, 1981), 62.
2. Robert A. Raines, *Success Is a Moving Target* (Waco: Word Books, 1979), 29.
3. "K" in Rippon's *A Selection of Hymns*, "How Firm A Foundation," in *The United Methodist Hymnal* (Nashville: The United Methodist Publishing House 1989), no. 529.

About the Author

KARLA M. KINCANNON, an artist and United Methodist minister, founded SpiritArt Ministries, an innovative spiritual direction practice to serve individuals and groups through the healing arts. Karla earned a BA in art from Virginia Wesleyan College and an MDiv from Garrett-Evangelical Theological Seminary in Evanston, Illinois.

A former campus minister, Karla taught religion courses at the college level. The author of numerous articles about the spiritual journey, she lectures, leads workshops, and facilitates retreats in a variety of ecumenical settings nationwide. She lives in east Tennessee with her husband, the Reverend Dr. Jim Noseworthy.

Other Titles of Interest
from Upper Room Books®

ABUNDANCE: JOYFUL LIVING IN CHRIST
by Marilyn Brown Oden
ISBN 0-8358-0822-X

CREATING A LIFE WITH GOD:
THE CALL OF ANCIENT PRAYER PRACTICES
by Daniel Wolpert
ISBN 0-8358-9855-5

JESUS, OUR SPIRITUAL DIRECTOR:
A PILGRIMAGE THROUGH THE GOSPELS
by Wendy Miller
ISBN 0-8358-9876-8

PRAYER AND OUR BODIES
by Flora Slosson Wuellner
ISBN 0-8358-0568-9

Visit your local bookstore
Call toll free 1-800-972-0433
Order online at www.upperroom.org/bookstore